D1190662

STUDIES IN
Organization Design

THE IRWIN-DORSEY SERIES IN BEHAVIORAL SCIENCE

EDITOR   JOHN F. MEE   *Indiana University*

ARGYRIS   *Interpersonal Competence and Organizational Effectiveness*

ARGYRIS   *Organization and Innovation*

CARZO & YANOUZAS   *Formal Organization: A Systems Approach*

CUMMINGS & SCOTT   *Readings in Organizational Behavior and Human Performance*

GUEST   *Organizational Change: The Effect of Successful Leadership*

KELLY   *Organizational Behaviour*

KUHN   *The Study of Society: A Unified Approach*

LAWRENCE & SEILER, WITH BAILEY, KATZ, ORTH, CLARK, BARNES, & TURNER   *Organizational Behavior and Administration: Cases, Concepts, and Research Findings*   rev. ed.

LORSCH & LAWRENCE (eds.)   *Studies in Organization Design*

LYNTON & PAREEK   *Training for Development*

MASLOW   *Eupsychian Management: A Journal*

MASSARIK & RATOOSH   *Mathematical Explorations in Behavioral Science*

O'CONNELL   *Managing Organizational Innovation*

ORTH, BAILEY, & WOLEK   *Administering Research and Development: The Behavior of Scientists and Engineers in Organizations*

PORTER & LAWLER   *Managerial Attitudes and Performance*

PRICE   *Organizational Effectiveness: An Inventory of Propositions*

RUBENSTEIN & HABERSTROH (eds.)   *Some Theories of Organization*   rev. ed.

SCOTT   *The Management of Conflict*

SEILER   *Systems Analysis in Organizational Behavior*

WHYTE   *Organizational Behavior: Theory and Application*

WHYTE & HAMILTON   *Action Research for Management*

STUDIES IN

Organization
Design

Edited by

Jay W. Lorsch, D.B.A.
*Associate Professor of Organizational
Behavior*

and

Paul R. Lawrence, D.C.S.
*Wallace Brett Donham Professor of
Organizational Behavior*

*Both of the
Graduate School of Business Administration
Harvard University*

1970
RICHARD D. IRWIN, INC.
AND
THE DORSEY PRESS

HOMEWOOD, ILLINOIS

IRWIN-DORSEY LIMITED, GEORGETOWN, ONTARIO

First Printing, February, 1970

Library of Congress Catalog Card No. 77–015915

Printed in the United States of America

Foreword

Cᴏɴᴛʀᴀʀʏ to popular belief, the editors of a collection of papers such as this do serve certain useful purposes. First, they must come up with an idea or theme for the book. In this case, there were really several ideas which stimulated us to develop this volume. A major concern was the fact that all too often interesting pieces of research by young scholars remain buried in archives and never reach the audience of other researchers who may be interested in them or practitioners who might apply them. By putting together these papers, many of which are outgrowths of doctoral theses at the Harvard Business School, we hoped to bring them into wider circulation. But, as the reader will learn from the introductory chapter, many of these papers also share a common characteristic of elaborating on our own work in a direction which we hope will continue to evolve. In fact, Lawrence was the thesis chairman for Burns and Ruedi, while Lorsch was thesis chairman for Allen, Walker, and Morse. We are indebted to our colleagues David Moment (now at Boston College) and Richard Vancil because of their roles as thesis chairmen for Fisher and Athreya, respectively.

Another useful activity the editors can perform is to select a title. In this case we were torn between the possibility of using either a title which emphasized the conceptual thrust of this book or one which focused on the application of this work to practical problems. Because of another idea which led us to collect these papers, we chose the second alternative—to highlight in the title the implications of these studies for organization design. By organization design we mean the systematic planning of organization structures and practices. For too long, managers have had inadequate tools for reaching decisions about the design of organizations, and we feel these studies individually and collectively contain interesting approaches to these problems. They develop a conceptual model which can be useful to the practitioner in thinking about the social architecture of organizations in relation to the tasks they must perform. While to some readers such an assertion may smack of manipulation without regard to hu-

v

man values, we would only ask that the reader so concerned peruse Morse's paper. His findings clearly suggest that attention to organization design in relation to the task to be performed can also result in important psychological benefits for the organization's members.

Another function the editors can perform is to select and organize the papers. Our rationale for this is explained in Chapter 1. In addition, we have written a brief note preceding each paper to help the reader place it in the context of the author and his interests.

Finally, the editors can also acknowledge for themselves and the various authors the contributions of others who have helped to make these papers possible. In this respect, in addition to our colleagues already mentioned, we would like to thank Bertrand Fox, former Director, and Lawrence Fouraker, Director, of the Division of Research of the Harvard Business School, for their help in financially supporting the thesis activity of Allen, Fisher, Morse, Ruedi, and Walker. Much of this support came from the Associates of the Harvard Business School and we are grateful to these firms.

Many of these studies were conducted in business firms. For the various authors we would like to express their thanks to managers and personnel of these firms who must necessarily remain anonymous.

We would also like to thank the American Academy of Management for permission to use the Udy paper and the Harvard Business Review for permission to reprint the Walker and Lorsch articles. The Motivation Research Group kindly gave us permission to use the Climate Profile in the Ruedi and Lawrence paper.

We are indebted to Miss Jeanne Deschamps for her careful editing of these papers. Her work on them has proved to us that editing can be a creative activity. Finally, we would like to thank Mrs. Ann Walter who patiently typed and retyped many of these papers through their several versions.

Cambridge, Massachusetts　　　　　　　　　　JWL
January, 1970　　　　　　　　　　　　　　　　　PRL

Contents

1 | An Orientation and Introduction

During the past few years there has been evident a new trend in the study of organizational phenomena. Underlying this new approach is the idea that the internal functioning of organizations must be consistent with the demands of the organization task, technology, or external environment, and the needs of its members if the organization is to be effective.[1] Rather than searching for the panacea of the one best way to organize under all conditions, investigators have more and more tended to examine the functioning of organizations in relation to the needs of their particular members and the external pressures facing them. Basically, this approach seems to be leading to the development of a "contingency" theory of organization with the appropriate internal states and processes of the organization contingent upon external requirements and member needs.[2] To put it more succinctly, as Burns and Stalker have found, the organizational pattern necessary to operate in the electronics industry is not appropriate to doing business in manufacturing textile equipment and vice versa.[3]

This general trend has been accompanied by two less visible, but important tendencies in the study of organization. First, is the general approach of studying organizations as systems of variables interacting with their environment. Second is the increasing tendency to

---

[1] See for example such books as Paul R. Lawrence and Jay W. Lorsch, *Organization and Environment: Managing Differentiation and Integration* (Boston: Division of Research, Harvard University Graduate School of Business Administration, 1967); James S. Thompson, *Organizations in Action* (New York: McGraw-Hill, 1968); Joan Woodward, *Industrial Organization: Theory and Practice* (London: Oxford University Press, 1965); Tom Burns and G. M. Stalker, *The Management of Innovation* (London: Tavistock Publications, 1961); Victor H. Vroom, *Work and Motivation* (New York: John Wiley & Sons, Inc., 1964); Fred E. Fiedler, *A Theory of Leadership Effectiveness* (New York: McGraw-Hill, 1967).

[2] For a fuller elaboration, see Lawrence and Lorsch, *ibid.*

[3] Burns and Stalker, *op. cit.*

1

undertake applied research—that is, studies which not only are intended to generate increased understanding about organizational functioning but which also are supposed to throw light on the practical problems of administrators. That these two trends should emerge together is not surprising. Once researchers begin to view organizations as whole systems, they are placing themselves in a perspective similar to the manager who must administer the organization. They can view the whole "ball of wax" and can consider what the practical implications of their research may be.

We should recognize that these applied research studies often are written in a behavioral science jargon and are complicated. For these reasons they are often difficult for the practitioner to understand easily. But, in spite of these shortcomings (which we have attempted to minimize to some extent in the studies reported here), we believe that applied research offers a more useful basis for helping managers deal with organizational issues than the more readable and less complicated reporting of one man's observations or theorizing, which so often characterize the typical managerial "how to do it" book.

The purpose of this volume, then, is to bring to the attention of practicing managers and students of administration these three trends —toward a contingency theory of organization, toward studying organizations as systems, and toward applied research. They are the central themes which intellectually bind the chapters of this book together. Obviously, because many of the contributors have worked with the editors, the particular brand of contingency theory which is most heavily represented is derived from our earlier work, *Organization and Environment*.[4] Yet certain of the pieces draw heavily on other approaches to contingency theory. For example, Udy, who has been a major contributor to the development of contingency theory in his own right, develops further his own ideas.[5] Galbraith draws heavily on the formulations of Thompson.[6] All of these pieces regardless of their intellectual heritage, implicitly or explicitly use a systemic model as their underlying conceptual framework. With only minor exceptions, they all also represent applied research.

This last point is particularly important to the editors, because it is

---

[4] Lawrence and Lorsch, *op. cit.*

[5] Stanley H. Udy, *Organization of Work* (New Haven, Conn.: Human Relations Area File Press, 1959).

[6] Thompson, *op. cit.*

our hope that this book will not only strengthen the trend toward an increased awareness of contingency studies of organizations and more research in this direction but especially will provide for the practitioner some immediate ideas about how the results of this line of research can contribute to the solution of his current problems. Toward this latter end, the pieces included in this volume have been selected to cover a broad range of current managerial issues.

Managerial Issues

The first piece in the book by Allen focuses on the problems of corporate divisional relationships in the so-called conglomerate companies. Basically, he is concerned with how such companies must organize to permit the diversity necessary to deal with their broad range of businesses and products while still achieving the coordination or integration required to hold the whole enterprise together. While this study may be particularly interesting to managers involved in highly diversified companies, it also has relevance for the many managers concerned with administering and designing organizations for any multidivisional firm.

Walker and Lorsch's paper deals with a major organizational dilemma facing managers as they think about the basic structure of their organization. Should activities be aligned on a functional or a product basis? The authors do not offer any simple answer, but instead, provide some research findings which should help practitioners to understand more intelligently the tradeoffs inherent in this choice.

The chapter by Ruedi and Lawrence compares a German organization with American firms, all of which are operating in the plastics industry. This study provides an understanding of the relationship between organization, the business environment, and culture. To the manager involved in multinational business with facilities in different cultures, this article should provide important understanding about the problems of carrying organizational practices from one country to another.

A pervasive managerial issue is addressed by Morse in reporting the results of his study, which focuses on the interface between the individual and the organization. Given the task of a functional unit —such as a research laboratory or a manufacturing plant—how should it be structured to motivate personnel to work effectively? Can managers design and develop organizations which simultaneously meet the needs of individual members and the requirements of the unit's work?

Galbraith reports on a study which examines the problems of coordination or integration in an organization working on a complex and highly interdependent technical program. His findings are particularly relevant to the increasing number of administrators concerned with designing and managing organizations for such programs. What methods are available to achieve integration, and under what conditions are various methods (program offices, schedules, task forces) appropriate?

Program offices, as one important integrating device, are the focus of Burns's study. He examines the internal structural pattern of program offices and how this seems to facilitate their integrative role. He also examines their position in the total organization and the types of organizational settings which are conducive to their effectiveness. His findings also should be of particular interest to managers concerned with managing complex technical programs.

Fisher also examines a particular type of integrative device present in many business organizations—the product manager. His emphasis is on the psychological characteristics and behavioral patterns which are necessary to be effective in such positions. What are the problems of living in such positions and of managing those who do? While the subjects of this study are product managers in a consumer products company, the implications would seem to hold for personnel in similar coordination roles in other types of organizations—e.g., program managers, business managers, venture managers, etc.

Long-range planning is the subject of Athreya's study. Recognizing that one of the important functions of long-range planning is to integrate the various organizations' units, he examines the characteristics of effective and less-effective planning departments. His findings suggest certain characteristics of an effective planning department and provide useful insights both to managers in the planning function and to those concerned with the establishment and design of an effective planning function.

In this review of the managerial issues covered in this volume, we have not mentioned the chapters by Udy or Hampden-Turner because, strictly speaking, they are not applied studies. Yet it would be misleading to suggest that they do not have relevance to practicing managers. Udy provides an interesting explanation of why the basic division of labor among sales, production, and research functions exists in modern business firms. Hampden-Turner focuses on the individual personality and theorizes about the individual characteristics which are necessary for the effective manager. But the major reason for including these two chapters is the light they shed and the use they make of the concepts of differentiation and integration which underly the other pieces. This will become more apparent as we examine the particular version of contingency theory in which most of these studies are rooted.

The Basic Model of Organization

As we have indicated above, most of these studies build on or are related to the particular contingency model which we developed in *Organization and Environment.*[7] As the next step in orienting the reader to the chapters which follow, we wish to review the findings of this study briefly and also to indicate where the various pieces included in this volume suggest modifications or elaboration of them.

The basic contingent relationship on which our earlier work focused is that between an organization and its particular environment. To understand how the nature of a particular environment is related to the internal characteristics of the organization, it is necessary to first describe how we conceive of the environment. First, we have recognized that an organization operating in a single industry (in the case of our study, plastics, foods, or containers) segments its environment into three basic parts—market information, scientific information, and techno-economic (manufacturing) data—by assigning the task of coping with these factors to different functional units. Although we might earlier have argued that such a division of labor was due to the conventional wisdom of business managers, Udy's paper suggests that there are deeper historical and social reasons for this. In any case, because of this division of activity in dealing with the parts of the environment, each of these basic functional units must deal with a part of the environment which is more or less certain than the other parts. Various parts of the environment have different rates of change of information, different time span of feedback about results, and different certainty of information at a particular point in time. For example, a research unit in a particular environment may be

---

[7] Lawrence and Lorsch, *op. cit.*

confronted with rapid change, long-term feedback about results, and low certainty of information about the current state of knowledge. Its part of the environment would be characterized as highly uncertain. In contrast, a manufacturing unit in the same organization might be facing relatively little change, rapid feedback about results, and clear information about the current situation. Consequently, its part of the environment would be very certain.

Not only do different parts of the same environment vary along this certainty-uncertainty continuum, there are also variations among various industry environments. For example, in the plastics industry there was a highly uncertain scientific part of the environment, a highly certain techno-economic part, and a moderately uncertain market. Where, as in the plastics example, there is a wide range of uncertainty among parts of the environment, the total environment can be characterized as *diverse*. In contrast, where the parts of the environment fall close together on the certainty-uncertainty continuum, the environment is characterized as homogeneous. This was the case in the container industry, where the scientific, techno-economic, and market parts of the environment were all relatively certain.

The relative certainty of the parts of the environment and their resulting diversity or homogeneity was found to be related to one important characteristic of the organization—the *degree of differentiation* among its functional units. *By differentiation we mean the differences in cognitive and emotional orientation among managers in different units and the differences in formal structure among units.*

Specifically, differentiation among units was measured in terms of these four dimensions:

1. The formality of structure (e.g., high reliance on formal rules, procedures, and tight spans of control vs. the opposite conditions).
2. Goal orientation (concern with market goals vs. concern with cost, quality, and efficiency goals vs. concern with scientific goals).
3. Time orientation (long term vs. short term).
4. Interpersonal orientation (for interpersonal contact—concern with getting on with the work vs. concern for relationships with others).

In the effective organizations in the original studies, functional units had structures and the members of these units had orientations which were consistent with the demands of their part of the environment.[8] For example, in a research laboratory in an effective plastics organization, managers and scientists had long-term time orientations, scientific goal orientations, task-oriented interpersonal relations, and the unit itself had a low degree of formal structure. This was consistent with the uncertain work of doing scientific investigation. On the other hand, in a sales unit in the same organization, the members had shorter time orientations, were oriented toward market goals, were relationship oriented in dealing with colleagues, and they worked in a unit with a moderate amount of structure. All of this was consistent with the requirements of their moderately uncertain task. In the less-effective organizations, the orientations of unit members and unit structure did not meet the demands of the various parts of the environment so well.

These findings suggest the first contingent relationship between the organization and its environment. Since each unit must fit the demands of its part of the environment, in diverse environments, the units tend to be more differentiated from each other than in homogeneous environments. The appropriate amount of differentiation is important to allow each unit to do its own "thing" but as we shall see it also contains the seeds of certain problems in achieving united effort.

The study by Morse throws further light on the importance of a functional unit having a structure and set of orientations consistent with its task environment. It suggests that one reason that this fit is important is that it is connected to the increased motivation of the personnel in the unit. Morse also suggests several other dimensions along which functional units must be differentiated if they are to meet the demands of their respective parts of the environment.

While the original work focused only on differentiation among major functional units, Walker and Lorsch have found that differentiation is also present within such units (in this case, manufacturing plants). They also report that the degree of differentiation can be influenced by whether the work within the functional unit is further divided according to functional specialty (quality control, maintenance, etc.) or by product manufactured. Similarly, Allen has found that differentiation also is present between the corporate headquarters and operating divisions of large diversified firms. Such differentiation

---

[8] The term effective is used here, as in the study, to mean effectiveness in economic terms, i.e., growth in profits, sales volume, and return on investment.

is important for the headquarters to deal with its part of the total corporate environment and also for each division to deal effectively with its own business environment.

But the requirement for differentiation is only one of several issues posed by the environment. A second is the dominant competitive issue in the industry. In two of the industries studied originally (plastics and consumer food products), the dominant competitive issue was innovating new products and processes. In the third industry studied (the container industry) the dominant issue was the scheduling and allocation of production facilities to meet market demands. The dominant competitive issue is important because it is related to the final environmental requirement which has concerned us—*the pattern and degree of or integration required among units.* By integration we mean unity of effort among units, and we shall use the term interdependent as a synonym.

In the three industries originally studied, the tightness of integration required among units was found to be similar. However, there was an important difference in the pattern of units around which this integration was required. In the two industries where the dominant competitive issue was innovation (foods and plastics), the tight interdependence was required between sales and research on the one hand and production and research units on the other. In the container industry, with the issue of scheduling and allocating manufacturing facilities dominant, the tight interdependence was required only between production and sales.

In all three industries, it was found that the effective organizations achieved better integration among the units requiring a degree of interdependence than did their less-effective competitors. However, these high performing organizations were also achieving greater differentiation among those same units. This is important to stress for two reasons. First, it points to the basic demands of the environment that an organization must meet—for both differentiation and integration. Second, and related to this, it directs attention to the fundamental organizational issue which must be managed if an organization is to be successful—how to get simultaneously both differentiation and integration. For within any one organization it was found that these two states were basically antagonistic. The more different any two highly interdependent units were in members' orientations and/or structure, the more problems there were of achieving integration.

In essence, what we found was that organizations, to be economically successful, needed to meet environmental demands for both differentiation and integration, but they had to do this in spite of the fact that these two states were opposed to each other. The more different two highly interdependent units were, the more difficult it was for their members to communicate with the understanding necessary to achieve satisfactory integration. As Hampden-Turner points out in his intriguing paper on human personality, the act of achieving differentiation and integration is an example of synergy—making the whole greater than the sum of its parts.

Allen amplified these original findings by pointing out that, in the corporate-divisional relationships he studied, this inverse relationship between differentiation and integration was affected by the relative performance standing of the division in the company. In the original study this inverse relationship was found only among units which were required to be highly interdependent. Allen found in corporate-divisional relationships that such required interdependence was related to the economic performance of the division. If a division was doing well, neither corporate management nor the divisional executives felt the need for integration very highly.[9] Everything was going well so the unit could be treated relatively independently. However, when a division was having economic difficulties, the need for integration was felt more strongly because then corporate and divisional management had to work together to solve problems. Only when there was low performance and the resulting requirement to fight integration did Allen find the inverse relationship between differentiation and integration. This together with the original should suggest that differences in outlook can be solved in an organization, as long as tight integration is not an issue.

But in many organizations, among certain units, the issue of achieving the synergy of differentiation and integration is crucial because in those interunit relations there is both a need for differentiation and for integration. How then do organizations achieve both differentiation and integration? The original study suggests two factors which are important. First, the structural devices used to achieve integration and, second, the patterns of behavior used to manage interdepartmental conflict.

Looking first at the structural devices used to achieve integration, it

---

[9] This point is closely related to March and Simon's emphasis on the importance of the "felt need" for joint decision making. James March and Herbert Simon, *Organizations* (New York: John Wiley & Sons, Inc., 1958).

was found that these seemed to vary with the amount of differentiation in the organization. In the organizations in the plastics industry, there was the most complicated array of integrating devices—entire departments of integrating personnel, cross-functional teams, the management hierarchy itself, as well as paper systems and schedules. In fact, in each of six plastics organizations studied about 22 of all management personnel were involved as special integrators. In the two food companies where somewhat less differentiation was required these integration devices were somewhat less complex, with less reliance on either teams or integrating departments. In each of these organizations, 17 percent of the managerial personnel occupied special integrating roles. In the container industry where less differentiation was required all the integration could be handled through the managerial hierarchy and paper schedules. No other integrating devices seemed to be necessary. It is important to emphasize that, in general, the same types of integrating devices existed in economically effective and less-effective companies. This suggests that these devices were necessary to achieve both integration and differentiation but not sufficient by themselves to account for the variations in the extent to which these organizations met the demands posed by the environment.

Before we turn to the management of conflict which did help to account for why some organizations met the demand for both differentiation and integration while others did not, it is helpful to point to how some of the papers in this volume have contributed more to our understanding of the appropriate selection of integrative devices. As suggested above, our original idea was that such devices should be tailored to the requirement for differentiation. However, the theorizing of Thompson contributed to our own understanding of this issue and influenced Allen and Galbraith in their studies.[10]

According to Thompson, there are three types of interdependence:

Pooled—where each part renders a discrete contribution to the whole and each is supported by the whole, but no direct interaction is required between the units of the organization.
Sequential—when "direct interdependence can be pinpointed between them (the units) and the order of the interdependence can be specified." This interdependence is "not symmetrical."

---

[10] Thompson, op. cit.

Reciprocal—when "the outputs of each (unit) become the inputs for the others" . . . "under conditions of reciprocal interdependence each unit involved is penetrated by the others."

Thompson further suggests that there is a relationship between the types of interdependence required by the organization's environment and the integrative devices needed in the organization. For pooled interdependence more reliance can be put on establishing standard decision rules and procedures. Where sequential interdependence is required integration must be achieved by plan. Reciprocal interdependence requires that integration be achieved through mutual adjustment. That is, by face-to-face contact, which implies the use of individual integrators or cross-functional teams, etc.

In reviewing our original data we recognized that there was a difference in the type of interdependence between the plastics and food industries on the one hand and the container industry on the other. In the plastics and food industries, a reciprocal interdependence was required between sales-research and production-research. This *plus* the required differentiation seemed to generate a need for the more complex integrative devices found in the organizations in these industries. In the container industry where the dominant issue was scheduling, the interdependence was of the pooled and sequential types. It was sequential in that sales specified requirements for production, but it was pooled in that allocation decisions had to be made with regard to scarce production capacity. The simpler type of required interdependence and the lower degree of differentiation required of organizations in this business meant that the simpler integrative devices were adequate.

The studies of Allen and Galbraith also build on Thompson's ideas. Allen points out that at the corporate-divisional level of diversified companies only pooled interdependence is required, which means that simple integrative mechanisms, such as plans and the hierarchy, are sufficient. Galbraith devotes almost exclusive attention to these three types of interdependence and to the various integrative devices used to deal with them in the aerospace firm he studied. His data seem to substantiate much of Thompson's theory.

We should also indicate that several other of these studies also focus on integrative devices of various sorts. Athreya has studied the long-range planning process as an integrative device. Burns focuses on program offices, which are a most complicated integrative mechanism, while Fisher examines the role of product manager, another type of integrator. Walker and Lorsch examine how the arrangement of the management hierarchy, which is *the* traditional integrative device, can affect differentiation and integration. Finally, Ruedi and Lawrence explore how integrative devices used in U.S. and German plastics organizations fit both the requirements of the environment and the expectations of the two cultures.

We now want to return to the management of conflict, which is the most important factor accounting for whether organizations achieve the synergy of differentiation and integration. Conflict management is important to achieving differentiation and integration because differentiation by its very nature seems to imply conflict. When persons have to work together but have different views about the problem—which is what the concept of differentiation is all about —they are going to have a conflict. If they are going to have productive collaboration or integration, they must somehow resolve that conflict. In the original study, it was found that the firms which achieved the differentiation and integration required by the environment were those whose members effectively resolved conflict.

A constellation of factors were found to contribute to effective resolution of conflict. First was the confrontation of conflict. In the effective organization, rather than smoothing over differences or using power to win a point, the managers openly discussed their differences and worked until a sound solution was found. Second, the pattern of influence or power, both among units and up and down the hierarchy, was found to be important. In essence, in the effective organization, the real decision-making influence was concentrated in those units and at those levels where the knowledge about the factors affecting decisions was also located. Third, in those organizations employing special integrative roles, it was found that these integrators needed to have a balanced orientation and viewpoint between the extremes of the units they were linking. These integrators were also more effective when they felt they were mostly rewarded for the total performance of the product group for which they were responsible.

Many of the studies reported here also deal with these conflict management variables. Burns deals with them in and around program offices. Allen examines how they operate in hierarchical relationships between the corporate headquarters and its divisions and adds the additional variable of the quantity and quality of communication up and down the hierarchy. Walker and Lorsch examine how conflict management is affected by the product versus functional choice. Athreya reports on how they are related to effective long-range planning, while Ruedi and Lawrence point up the impact of culture on the way conflict is handled. Finally, Fisher suggests some of the personal characteristics and behavior patterns required for integrators to work effectively at resolving conflict.

We have now presented the basic ideas which underly many of the studies reported here and how these newer findings relate to our original conclusions. One way to summarize these ideas is to refer to the sequence in which the studies are presented. The chapters by Allen, Walker and Lorsch, and Ruedi and Lawrence are presented first, because they provide an overview of the full set of concepts. They each deal with the requirements for differentiation, integration, and conflict management in different settings—Allen in the hierarchical relationship between corporate headquarters and divisions in diversified firms; Walker and Lorsch within two production plants in two large consumer products companies; Ruedi and Lawrence in U.S. and German organizations. The reader who is still unsure of the basic concepts and their interrelationship will find that any or all of these pieces will aid his understanding as well as provide fresh insights into the managerial problems they address. The articles by Morse and by Udy focus on the issue of differentiation—why it is important and its historical derivation. The pieces by Galbraith, Burns, Fisher, and Athreya are concerned with various types of integrative devices and the issues of conflict management to make these devices effective in achieving both differentiation and integration. Finally, the piece by Hampden-Turner departs from the others as he uses the concepts of differentiation and integration to examine the human personality. But, in another sense, this piece is basic to all the others, because it raises the issue of the synergistic consequences of achieving differentiation and integration. Obtaining both requires human effort, but without both, the sum is no more than the parts of the organization, and the essence of organized work is to help people together to accomplish work more efficiently and meaningfully than they could as a collection of individuals.

Another aim of this book is to encourage others to study how to make human organizations more efficient as well as more meaningful places to work. Thus in closing this introductory chapter, we wish to touch briefly on possible future lines of research and the prospects for their broader utility.

Future Research and Research Applications

This volume is witness to the fact that the line of research the authors initiated with the original work published in *Organization and Environment* is continuing.[11] It has proved difficult to bring this book to press because of the temptation to wait for the inclusion of other studies in process. We seem to be in the pleasant but frantic state of seeing more interesting additional research leads than are immediately manageable. This is, undoubtedly, in many ways a product of our times, since organization studies, in general, are proving to have high relevance to many of our contemporary societal difficulties. Consider the range of problem areas in which organizational issues are being mentioned as pivotal. The crisis of our secondary educational system is being diagnosed by a number of observers as primarily an organizational problem.[12] Many commentators on the current troubles in higher education are likewise pointing to outmoded systems of governance as crucial. Hospitals are beset with organizational difficulties as they grapple with new technology and the need for more complex health delivery services. Many students of government are turning to an examination of organizational variables as leads to closing the gap between the goals of government programs and the results. Even the stubborn problems of our core cities are increasingly being seen as organizational in many respects.[13] These are all areas in which opportunities exist for doing research of the general type reported in this volume, but in institutional settings other than business.

A second general type of future research could be to follow up on the leads presented in the chapter by Morse. This study is a beginning toward building fresh research linkages between the study of organizations as total systems and the study of the individual in the organization. Recent studies, such as those reported by Schroder,[14] have found the twin concepts of differentiation and integration especially fruitful in understanding individual cognitive processes. This parallel line of

---

[11] *Op. cit.*

[12] See especially Anthony Ottinger, *Run Computer Run* (Cambridge, Mass.: Harvard University Press, 1969).

[13] See especially Richard Rosenbloom and Robin Marris, eds., *Social Innovation in the City*, Harvard University Program on Technology and Society (Cambridge, Mass.: Harvard University Press, 1969).

[14] Harold M. Schroder, Michael J. Driver, and Siegfried Streufert, *Human Information Processing* (New York: Holt, Rinehart & Winston, Inc., 1967).

work presents one challenge for finding empirical and conceptual connections.

There is also a slowly growing research interest in studying interorganization relations as a single system or network that crisscrosses the old boundaries we have drawn between the private and public sectors of the economy. One such study by Borchardt[15] of the telecommunication industry has drawn on the differentiation and integration framework to help describe and explain the evolution of this industry with its complex interplay between private firms, regulated utilities, and government agencies. Similar inquiries could prove fruitful in enhancing our understanding, not just our fears, of other modern "complexes."

The approach to cross-cultural research evidenced in the Ruedi-Lawrence piece opens up other possible lines of future research. It would be particularly intriguing to pursue this type of work in organizations in less-industralized cultures of various sorts. It might also be fruitful to evident similar studies in organizations operating in several cultures.

We mentioned earlier that one advantage of employing a systematic analysis of organizations is that it automatically tends to close the often overwhelming gap between basic organization research and the problems and concerns of organization managers. The reader can judge for himself in the chapters that follow whether the editors' optimism in this regard is justified. To the extent that it is, the further pursuit of research topics such as those sketched above should have payouts for practitioners—whether in school systems, hospitals, government agencies, multinational organizations, or businesses. Perhaps our society's obvious need for more effective organizations is distorting the authors' perceptions of what is possible. The pursuit of knowledge through research and its application in practice remains a difficult, risky, and time-consuming process. But clearly our times do create an urgency about both generating more understanding of organizations and widely disseminating and applying this knowledge. We need to perceive the potential of organizations as flexible tools expressly designed to serve our expanding human aspirations. This is an imperative for both practicing administrators and students of organization. Only as we can clearly see this possibility can we muster the will and the skill to make it a reality.

---

[15] Kurt Borchardt, *Structure and Performance of the U.S. Communications Industry: Government Regulation and Company Planning* (Boston: Division of Research, Harvard University Graduate School of Business Administration, in press).

2 | Corporate-Divisional Relationships in Highly Diversified Firms*

Stephen A. Allen III

In this chapter Allen takes a look at the newest form of corporate organization, the so-called conglomerate. His particular focus is on the crucial organizational issue which makes these diversified companies different from other large industrial enterprises: How to achieve financial and managerial control and coordination over diverse divisions while allowing them sufficient autonomy to operate in their respective industries. This paper is based on Allen's doctoral thesis at the Harvard Business School for which he won the McKinsey Foundation Post-Doctoral Fellowship for 1968. It was a comparative study of the corporate-divisional relations in two highly diversified companies. At the present time Allen, who is Assistant Professor of Organizational Behavior at the Harvard Business School, is involved with Professor Lorsch in an extension of this research into four other diversified organizations.

ONE of the more arresting and controversial developments witnessed by U.S. business during the past 15 years has been the rapid proliferation of the highly diversified, multi-divisional corporate form. If we treat involvement in five or more industry categories as a criterion of diversity, then approximately one-third of the *Fortune* 500 can be called diversified companies.[1] Much of the rapidity with which

---

* The findings upon which this chapter is based are reported in S. A. Allen, "Managing Organizational Diversity: A Comparative Study of Corporate-Divisional Relations" (unpublished doctoral thesis, Harvard Business School, 1968).

[1] This statement is based on data presented in Thomas O'Hanlan, "The Odd News about Conglomerates," *Fortune*, June 15, 1967, pp. 175–77. Five industry categories is an arbitrary criterion of diversity. At the same time it should be held in mind that a single industry category may contain a number of product-market segments, each of which may in turn require quite unique marketing and technological skills.

these diversifiers have risen to prominence must be attributed to their extensive use of acquisition and merger as a vehicle for obtaining almost instantaneous involvement in unfamiliar fields. Thus, during 1967 the annual rate of mergers reported by the Federal Trade Commission reached an all time high of 2,384. The FTC data also indicate that approximately 70% of the mergers consummated between 1960 and 1967 were of the conglomerate or multi-industry variety.

While diversification has become a way of life for an increasing number of companies, it has also presented their managements with some exceedingly difficult organizational problems. One needn't look very far to secure an indication of the importance of these problems. The business press has cited numerous examples where painstaking study and redesign of existing organizational schemes has been necessary before corporations could adequately capitalize on the potential inherent in their widespread operations. Similarly, data from three independent studies suggest that the overall failure rate among mergers approaches 25%.[2] Finally, published records of corporate performance show a wide range of variation among highly diversified firms; and one cause for this variation would seem to be that some of these firms have dealt with their organizational problems far better than others.

Although the payoff for knowledge concerning appropriate means of managing highly diverse, multi-divisional companies seems extremely high, surprisingly little systematic research has been conducted to determine what sorts of organizational arrangements are associated with effective coordination and with high financial performance in this particular corporate form. The findings reported in this chapter represent one attempt to shed some much needed light on this pressing management problem.

The discussion which follows will focus on five key questions which are frequently asked by both the participants and observers of the diversification movement. These questions are:

How are conglomerates, or highly diversified firms,[3] different from other organizational forms?

---

[2] These studies are:
J. Bjorksten, "Merger Lemons," *Mergers and Acquisitions: The Journal of Corporate Venture*, Vol. 1, No. 1, (Fall, 1965); Booz, Allen and Hamilton, "Management of New Products," 1960; John Kitching, "Why Mergers Miscarry," *Harvard Business Review*, November–December, 1967.

[3] Although there is considerable disagreement concerning the precise definition of these terms, "conglomerate" and "highly diversified firm" will be used interchangeably in this chapter.

In what ways and to what extent do corporate headquarters and divisional management systems in diversified firms have to be differentiated from one another?

What problems do corporate headquarters and divisional managements face in achieving integration?

What sorts of decision-making and conflict resolution processes prove effective in achieving corporate-divisional integration?

What kinds of organizational problems are involved in achieving the synergistic $(2 + 2 = 5)$ effects which managers often point to in discussing their diversification programs?

Before launching into a discussion of these questions, it is necessary to consider how the research was designed and some of the salient characteristics of the firms which were studied. With this information in hand the reader can judge for himself how the findings may relate to the particular issues in which he is interested.

A COMPARATIVE STUDY OF TWO HIGHLY DIVERSIFIED FIRMS

This study was designed to provide a comparative analysis of the problems of achieving integration between the corporate headquarters unit and each of several product divisions in two highly diversified firms. Each company had annual sales of between $300 and $500 million; each had followed a strategy of related diversification in acquiring away from a stable or declining business; and each had 10 or more product divisions. Both firms operated mainly in the broad areas of producers' and consumers' durables. Although both were still acquiring other firms at a moderate rate, they also invested between $20 and $30 million annually in their existing divisions. The corporate staff of each firm numbered between 20 and 25 executives. The major difference between the two corporations was that one had a significantly higher performance record than the other.

Each firm consisted of a number of profit center divisions which had virtually no market or technological interdependence with their sister divisions. These product divisions possessed all of the major functional specialities necessary to carry on business in their particular industries (e.g., marketing, production, engineering), and they had the major influence in shaping the content and direction of the strategies they employed in competing within their own industries. At the same time, these product divisions were not fully autonomous in that they were obliged to secure approval from the corporate headquarters for both their business plans and for major expenditures of funds. Also, the extent of their autonomy depended upon their ability to contribute a "reasonable" level of profits to the corporation as a whole.

The major decision processes around which integration between the corporate headquarters' unit and the product divisions in each firm were required were the allocation of funds, business planning, and control over profit contribution. In other words, the issues around which corporate-divisional integration was required tended to be mainly economic in nature rather than having to do with marketing or technical problems. Since there was no significant market or technological interdependence among divisions, direct interdivisional coordination was not required.

Having briefly considered some of the major characteristics of the two research sites, it is important to consider the degree to which they are representative of the growing number of firms which have chosen diversification as a way of life. Of course, there is always a question of how and to what degree one can generalize from a sample of two, and this issue is particularly acute in the case of highly diversified firms. Indeed, taken as a group, these firms tend to exhibit as many differences as similarities. For instance, they may range from more traditional examples such as General Electric, Du Pont, and Westinghouse to the newer combines such as Litton, Textron, and ITT, which are rapidly acquiring companies in a wide range of industries. Between these two extremes lies a group of firms which have acquired units that are more akin to existing parts of their operations, e.g., Borg-Warner, AMF, FMC, and TRW. Each of these diversification strategies undoubtedly requires somewhat different organizational approaches. However, all of the firms cited above do devote considerable effort to the management of internal operations; and on this basis they are similar to the two research sites. In other words, in the selection of firms to be studied an explicit choice was made not to focus on those conglomerates which depend almost solely on financial transactions as a means of enhancing earnings per share.

Another way to discriminate among the diversifiers is that some have fairly large corporate staffs which become more heavily involved in marketing and technical issues. Others, due to the nature of their acquisitions, tend to be more heavily committed to nurturing interdivisional collaboration. However, *at the minimum* all conglomerates appear to be engaged in the same decision-making processes as those which characterized the two research sites—i.e., allocation of resources, business planning, and control over divisional profit contributions in diverse businesses.

Having placed the research sites in context, let us now return to the more general question of how conglomerates differ from other corporate forms.

HOW ARE CONGLOMERATES DIFFERENT?

Two distinguishing features of any corporate form are (1) the diversity of management problems faced by its primary subunits and (2) the complexity of the organizational devices it employs to achieve integration among these subunits. When we look at conglomerates along these two dimensions, we are confronted with a rather intriguing paradox. By definition conglomerates consist of a sizable number of primary subunits (divisions) which face very diverse management problems; and, yet, corporate-divisional integration in these firms is accomplished through comparatively simple organizational devices. In the two firms studied corporate-divisional integration was achieved through paper systems (e.g., plans, budgets, and funds requests) and relatively infrequent direct contact among the top three organizational levels (i.e., corporate and group executives and division general managers). Recent articles by the business press on Litton, Textron, Ogden, and other well-known diversifiers suggest that the arrangements found in the current study tend to be typical of most conglomerates. By way of contrast, however, Lawrence and Lorsch have recently reported that considerably more complex sets of devices were required to achieve interdepartmental coordination in the plastics, food, and container industries.[4] As a matter of fact, these authors hypothesize that the more diverse the primary subunits, the more complex the devices required to achieve integration.[5]

While the conglomerates' ability to manage diverse units with comparatively simple integrative devices is certainly one of their distinguishing features, it also seems a bit like "black magic." The underlying explanation for this seeming paradox is simply that the

---

[4] Paul R. Lawrence and Jay W. Lorsch, *Organization and Environment: Managing Differentiation and Integration* (Boston: Division of Research, Harvard Business School, 1967), pp. 137–40.

[5] *Ibid.*

conglomerates have designed and/or evolved organizational arrangements which tend to limit the interdependence among major units. The pattern of interunit relationships which typifies diversified firms closely approximates what Thompson[6] calls *pooled interdependence*, and it has three important characteristics:

1. *Major subunits tend to be self-contained to a considerable degree.* The basic organizational unit in conglomerates is the divisional profit center rather than the functional department. Thus, although the corporate office may provide certain staff services, each product division possesses nearly all of the operating and control functions necessary to do business in its particular industry.
2. *The main area of interdependence is between the product divisions and the corporate headquarters.* Subject to the constraints posed by overall corporate goals and resources, most divisions in a conglomerate can operate independently of their sister divisions. Thus, comparatively little direct interdivisional coordination is required.
3. *Product divisions enjoy considerable autonomy vis-à-vis the corporate headquarters.* Because of the number and broad range of industries encompassed by its product divisions, the corporation is obliged to permit them considerable autonomy in both strategy and operations. By and large, corporate control tends to be exercised through evaluation of the economic aspects of divisional plans, budgets and requests and through allocation of funds rather than through direct participation in formulating the divisions' product-market strategies.

By way of contrast, a prototypical single-industry company organized along functional lines is characterized by what Thompson[7] terms *reciprocal interdependence*. In this situation the outputs of each major subunit may represent inputs for every other subunit. Decision-making in this situation not only requires considerable interdepartmental coordination but also considerably more complex headquarters-departmental relationships. The corporate office tends to become directly involved in technical and marketing issues as well as the broader financial aspects of planning, budgeting, and resource allocation. Of course, reciprocal interdependence does exist among functional departments *within* the product divisions of a conglomerate; however, this more complex form of interdependence does not carry over to the level of corporate-divisional and interdivisional relationships.

---

[6] James D. Thompson, *Organizations in Action* (New York: McGraw-Hill Book Co., 1967), pp. 54–55.

[7] *Ibid.*

Pooled and reciprocal interdependence may be thought of as forming a spectrum of integrative requirements. The pooled interdependence which characterizes corporate-divisional relationships in conglomerates requires the least complex integrative devices, while the reciprocal interdependence of single product firms calls for the most complex integrative arrangements. Lying between these two extremes of integrative complexity are a number of other corporations which also have multi-divisional structures—e.g., pulp and paper manufacturers, consumer food companies, and major chemical firms. The lower diversity and technological characteristics of such firms, however, make their complex integrative arrangements more manageable.

To summarize, conglomerates have several organizational characteristics which make them a unique corporate form: diversity, comparatively simple integrative devices, pooled interdependence, major subunits which are both self-contained and autonomous to a considerable degree, and interunit coordinative requirements that center mainly around corporate-divisional relationships. Despite the fact that these firms have developed organizational arrangements which require less interdependence among major subunits, the problems of planning, budgeting, and resource allocation require a good deal of joint decision-making between corporate and divisional management systems. Achieving integration around these issues is no simple matter. At the same time, however, the findings of this study point to the conclusion that overall corporate performance is closely related to the ability to achieve both appropriate levels of corporate-divisional differentiation and high levels of corporate-divisional integration. Let us now consider each of these behavioral factors in its turn.

CORPORATE-DIVISIONAL DIFFERENTIATION

Both because of their positions in the organizational hierarchy and because of the nature of the tasks they performed, members of the corporate and divisional management systems in each research site tended to develop specialized working styles and mental processes. For one thing, corporate and divisional executives focused their attention on different segments of their firms' task environments. Corporate contacts with external groups and organizations centered mainly around stockholders, the financial community, potential merger candidates, and governmental agencies. By way of contrast, top level division personnel were concerned mainly with the external groups which affected their ability to develop, sell, and produce goods and services in their particular industries. Members of the corporate and divisional units also played different roles in the planning, budgeting, and resource allocation process. Corporate managers were concerned with allocating resources among a number of divisions, maintaining control over divisional profit contributions, and assessing the realism of divisional plans and budgets. Members of the divisional management systems, on the other hand, focused on devising plans to capitalize on the opportunities existing in their particular industries and on securing the funds from the corporate office which were required to translate these plans into action.

As a consequence of their differing environmental contacts and organizational roles, corporate and divisional managers in each firm exhibited very different cognitive orientations and working styles in making decisions. Three dimensions of differentiation were consistently found in both firms:

1. *Formality of Structure.* Corporate headquarters units were much less formal in their structure than were the divisions. In other words, they tended to depend less on formal rules, review results less frequently, have fewer formally stated goals, and have wider spans of control.
2. *Orientations toward Time.* The corporate offices tended to have longer time horizons than their divisions.
3. *Goal Orientations.* Although concern for financial goals was high among both corporate and divisional managers, there was a much heavier emphasis placed on them at the corporate level. There was considerable differentiation among corporate and divisional management systems in terms of the emphasis managers placed on non-financial goals. In both firms corporate executives indicated that they emphasized financial, marketing, manufacturing, and engineering/research goals, (in that order) in evaluating plans. Divisional managers, however, ranked these same goals in a manner that was consistent with the dominant strategic issues posed by their particular industries. For example, managers in a defense division ranked research goals as the most important criteria in their decisions, whereas executives in a producers' durables division ranked manufacturing goals as more important.

Interpersonal orientations of corporate and divisional managers were also measured along a task versus social continuum; however, no large or consistent differences were found.

While these specialized cognitive orientations and working styles were important for managers in accomplishing the primary tasks of their subunits, they also created potential problems for achieving integration around the issues of planning, budgeting, and resource allocation. Such differences in viewpoints could lead to conflicts which would have to be resolved if integration was to be achieved between the corporate and divisional levels. This point will be covered in more detail shortly, but first let us focus on the methods used to measure differentiation.

Both single and total corporate-divisional differentiation scores were computed for a sample of four divisions in each firm which were selected to represent the breadth of the firm's operations. These scores reflected relative differences among corporate and divisional management systems in terms of formality of structure; members' interpersonal, time, and goal orientations; and overall goal sets.[8] One firm (H-C Industries) was characterized by higher product-market diversity (17 divisions operating in very different industries), and it also exhibited higher corporate-divisional differentiation. The other firm (IPC) had lower product-market diversity (9 domestic divisions, some of which operated in segments of the same industry) and lower corporate-divisional differentiation. Although both firms were characterized by considerable corporate-divisional differentiation, we have seen that H-C Industries had a higher degree of differentiation than IPC; and this higher differentiation was related to the greater diversity of businesses in which H-C's divisions operated. Now let's consider what sort of problems each of the firms faced in achieving integration.

PROBLEMS OF ACHIEVING INTEGRATION

The data presented in Table 2.1 show under what conditions corporate-divisional integration tended to be most difficult to achieve in both of the research sites. Relationships between corporate headquarters units and divisional management systems at H-C and IPC are summarized in terms of four measures.[9] Differentiation scores, which were discussed in the preceding section, indicate the degree to which corporate and divisional managers diverge in their goals, work-

---

[8] For a more complete description of methodology, see S. A. Allen, "Managing Organizational Diversity: A Comparative Study of Corporate-Divisional Relations" (unpublished doctoral thesis, Harvard Business School, 1968), pp. 234–65.

[9] *Ibid.*

TABLE 2.1

Summary Measures of Corporate-Divisional Relationships*

Corporate-Divisional Relationships	Differentiation	Integration†	Effort Devoted to Integration	Divisional Performance‡
H-C$_I$ 20	5.14	31.9	High
H-C$_{II}$ 17	4.87	47.8	High
H-C$_{III}$ 20	3.56	121.0	Low
H-C$_{IV}$ 14	3.75	65.3	Low
IPC$_I$ 15	4.94	127.5	High
IPC$_{II}$ 9	4.33	134.7	High
IPC$_{III}$ 9	4.89	140.0	Low
IPC$_{IV}$ 8	2.62	189.4	Low

* Higher scores indicate greater differentiation, higher performance, more effective integration, and more effort devoted to achieving integration.
  Relationships among these measures are as follows:
  Spearman's coefficient of rank correlation between differentiation and integration is .39 (not significant) for 8 divisions.
  Coefficient of correlation between differentiation and integrative effort is −.84 (significant at .01 level, but in opposite direction from that predicted).
  Coefficient of correlation between integration and divisional performance is .80 (significant at .05 level) for 8 divisions.
  † Differences between scores for H-C$_I$ and H-C$_{II}$ and those for H-C$_{III}$ and H-C$_{IV}$ is significant at the .001 level (analysis of variance). Difference between scores for IPC$_I$ and IPC$_{III}$ and those for IPC$_{II}$ and IPC$_{IV}$ is also significant at .001 level. Difference between scores for H-C$_{III}$ and H-C$_{IV}$ and those for IPC$_{IV}$ is significant at .10 level.
  ‡ Differences between ratings for high performing pairs of divisions and low performing pairs at both H-C and IPC are significant at .001 level (analysis of variance).

ing styles, and orientations. Integration scores are based on corporate and divisional managers' ratings of the quality of collaboration actually achieved between the headquarters' unit and the managers' respective divisions. Divisional performance ratings are based on subjective estimates by corporate and divisional managers of sales, profit, and return on investment results over the most recent five years. (Rankings based on these estimates coincided with rankings based on actual figures which were available at H-C. Actual figures were not available for IPC.) The amount of effort devoted to achieving integration was determined by asking both corporate and divisional managers to rate the proportion of their working time over the past year which had been devoted to particular corporate-divisional relationships.

Although Lawrence and Lorsch's findings[10] would lead one to expect an inverse relationship between differentiation and integration, Table 2.1 indicates that in the current research sites there is no simple negative relationship between *degree* of differentiation and either the quality of integration actually achieved or the effort devoted to achiev-

[10] Lawrence and Lorsch, *op. cit.*, pp. 47–49.

ing integration. Among the high performers in each firm the more highly differentiated divisions are characterized by higher integration and lower integrative effort. This same relationship holds for IPC_{III} and IPC_{IV}. Only in the comparison of $H\text{-}C_{III}$ and $H\text{-}C_{IV}$ does the evidence show that higher differentiation is related to lower integration and greater integrative effort. Table 2.1 does, on the other hand, indicate a strong relationship between low performance, low integration, and more effort devoted to achieving integration.

The findings presented in Table 2.1 can be explained in terms of the broad organizational characteristics of IPC and H-C, and these characteristics appear to be fairly representative of most highly diversified firms. First of all, product divisions tend to be *conditionally autonomous*. That is to say, as long as a division meets its profit commitments to the corporation and presents no unexpected contingencies for the funds flow process, it requires only a minimal amount of supervision. Thus, as the data indicate, high performing divisions are characterized by higher integration and less effort devoted to achieving integration. One division general manager at IPC summarized the situation in this way:

A high profit contribution gives you a considerable "go to hell factor" in dealing with the headquarters people. But when you're losing, it's a whole new ball game. In fact, I'd say that the amount of supervision that a division receives is directly proportional to the trouble it's in. If you're meeting most of your objectives, and don't surprise corporate management too much, you're in fine shape. If you start missing budgets or request large amounts of capital, then, you've got to spend more time explaining your situation. When things get really bad, they send the staff in to make a study, whether you've invited them or not. All this is as it should be. We division managers are always great proponents of "splendid independence." But when a person is in trouble, he often loses his objectivity; and he needs somebody else to ask the right questions.

The small corporate headquarters units at H-C and IPC were consistent with the conditional autonomy enjoyed by product divisions. With only 20–25 executives at the corporate level, the headquarters units at H-C and IPC were obliged to manage by exception. Thus, the low performing divisions or those which posed significant contingencies for financial planning tended to receive the most corporate attention. The president of IPC described his firm's approach to corporate-divisional relations as follows:

Involvement on the part of the headquarters unit depends on who is having the biggest problems. We try to concentrate our shots rather than spreading our efforts equally among the nine divisions. We try to set priorities in allocating headquarters attention. Thus, we tend to get involved in those divisions where we think our efforts will have the greatest impact on ROI. This means that high performing divisions run fairly independently.

The foregoing discussion of the data in Table 2.1 points to the conclusion that corporate-divisional differentiation is only one of several factors affecting the quality of integration actually achieved between the headquarters' unit and its divisions. Differentiation appears to be an important factor only in those cases where low divisional performance or unanticipated changes in funds requirements lead to a greater felt-need for joint decision-making between the headquarters and a product division. This felt-need for joint decision-making is ultimately reflected in a greater effort devoted to achieving integration. Under these conditions, as in the settings studied by Lawrence and Lorsch, higher differentiation does make it more difficult to achieve integration. However, when the felt-need for joint decision-making is lower, the degree of differentation does not appear to affect corporate-divisional relationships.

So far the discussion has focused on problems of integration which were common to both H-C and IPC. The most intriguing findings of this study, however, revolve around differences between the two firms. These differences are summarized below.

TABLE 2.2

Summary Comparison of H-C and IPC

Variable	H-C	IPC
1. Product-market diversity	Higher	Lower
2. Overall differentiation	Higher	Lower
3. Overall integration	Higher	Lower
4. Overall integrative effort	Lower	Higher
5. Corporate performance (ROI, sales and profit growth)	Higher	Lower

H-C was at once more diverse and faced with higher total corporate-divisional differentiation. Yet, H-C was not only achieving higher overall integration but also devoting considerably less management effort to achieving this integration! At the same time, H-C had turned in a much higher level of financial performance than IPC for the most recent 5- and 10-year periods.

One reason for the different amounts of managerial effort devoted to integration was the differing management philosophies followed by H-C and IPC. H-C's corporate office favored a high degree of decentralization and depended on a fairly simple but highly selective set of organizational devices to maintain control over its divisions. IPC, on the other hand, sought considerably more involvement in planning, budgeting, and resource allocation; and it employed a more elaborate set of organizational devices to achieve this involvement. In other words, corporate-divisional integration at IPC entailed a higher felt need for joint decision-making.

Regardless of management philosophies, H-C was achieving higher integration. What was it about H-C's organizational system that allowed it to function so effectively?

FACTORS RELATED TO ACHIEVING HIGHER INTEGRATION

In designing this research several factors were identified which it was felt might be associated with the effective management of the conflicts that often arise between headquarters and divisional management systems around the issues of planning, budgeting, and resource allocation. In essence, it was predicted that higher integration would result in those cases where corporate and divisional managers were able to deal with conflicts in such a way that their decisions gave considerable weight to *both* the needs of the corporation for control and predictability of earnings and the demands placed on divisions by their task environments.

It was found that H-C Industries met six partial determinants of effective conflict resolution to a considerably greater extent than IPC. Each of the partial determinants which were associated with H-C's higher integration is listed below along with a brief discussion of why it seemed to be important:

1. *Intermediate Orientations and High Influence of Linking Functions.* One or more key management personnel were made responsible for mediating between the goals and concerns of the corporate office and those of each divisional management system. Depending on the particular division involved, these managers were either group executives, division general managers, or both. These executives tended to have

goal, time, and interpersonal orientations which were intermediate between those of the management systems they sought to link. They also possessed high influence relative to the two management systems that they bridged. It would seem that (*a*) a responsiveness to the needs of both management systems and (*b*) the ability to play a significant role in joint decision-making are necessary conditions for playing an effective integrative role.

2. *Influence Balance.*   A rough balance was maintained between the influence exerted by the corporate headquarters and by divisional managers over the joint decisions which affected future courses taken by the divisions. This factor seems to lie at the heart of successful delegation. In order to achieve a balance in influence, the corporate office had to be willing to allow the divisions considerable autonomy in pursuing opportunities in their respective industries. At the same time, the divisions had to be willing to accept constraints that the superordinate goals of the corporation might place on their abilities to move in certain directions. The important thing here was that the needs and desires of both parties tended to be given considerable weight. Single joint decisions did not necessarily satisfy the goals of each party to an equal degree; however, each party tended to be aware of the costs of the decision to the other party. Indeed, influence balance appeared to involve a sort of intangible "social accounting system" by which in the long run each party secured as many concessions as it gave. Also central to influence balance was the belief on the part of managers that joint decision-making was not a zero-sum-game, i.e., that concessions and influence were not scarce commodities where one party's gain was necessarily the other party's loss.

3. *Confrontation.*   Where outright conflicts were evident, they tended to be resolved more often at H-C by confronting the differences that arose and working them through rather than by forcing or smoothing. If either corporate headquarters or a division feels that it has been coerced into a joint decision, it is likely to leave the situation being less committed to making the decision work. Similarly, it will be less inclined to admit to any weaknesses that might exist in its position the next time a joint decision is under consideration. Where the goal is to test the efficacy of potential investment opportunities and to continually generate new opportunities, lack of confrontation can dampen the quality of the whole joint decision-making process.

4. *Evaluation and Reward Systems.*   Considerable attention was given by corporate management to insure that it was rewarding divisional managers on a basis which was congruent with the demands and opportunities posed by their particular task environments. This seemed clearly evident in the case of the relative emphasis which was placed on

long- versus short-run performance criteria. To the degree that the time emphasis of the evaluation system diverges from the time emphasis of the division's environment, the corporate office runs the risk of motivating managers to react to an artificial system rather than actual environmental opportunities. Such a divergence may have other undesirable effects on joint decision-making by signalling to divisional managers that the corporate office doesn't really understand their particular situation. At H-C the evaluation system was more consistent with the environmental conditions of the various divisions than at IPC.

5. *Upward and Downward Communications Flows.* It may seem somewhat superfluous to underscore the importance of a high quality of upward and downward information flows. However, the findings at IPC indicated that corporate management was relatively ambiguous about its goals, and this contributed to a significantly lower quality of downward communications (as rated by divisional managers). Annual or semi-annual meetings to discuss corporate goals (such as those employed by H-C) might have improved joint decision-making considerably. Another reason why downward communications were more problematic at IPC was that the headquarters unit appeared to be suffering from a communications overload. In other words, its evaluation and control procedures appeared to be terribly complex given the size of its corporate staff. This suggests that the headquarters in designing its control and information systems should be particularly aware of the burdens they can place on top level executives. The options are either to (*a*) devise more selective controls or (*b*) employ a larger corporate staff.

6. *Rapidity in Responding to Divisional Requests.* The corporate office was keenly aware of the opportunity costs which might be entailed in delays in responding to divisional requests—either favorably or unfavorably. At IPC there were less rapid responses by the corporate office, and this was related to less effective joint decision-making. This does not suggest that quality of evaluation be subordinated to increasing the throughput of requests processed. Rather, it seems important that the headquarters' unit develop organizational mechanisms for evaluation and approval of requests which entail as few people as necessary to insure the quality of decisions. For instance, 11 corporate officers at IPC played an important role in evaluation and approval of plans, budgets, and requests, while only 6 managers performed this task at H-C. There was no evidence that the 11 men of IPC produced any better investment decisions. Certainly they required more time to arrive at decisions.

In the preceding section it was noted that low performing divisions pose a much greater problem for corporate-divisional integration than high performers. A comparison of low performing divisions at H-C and IPC indicated that those at H-C met more of the determinants of effective conflict resolution and were experiencing higher integration than their counterparts at IPC. This is further evidence of the importance of effective conflict resolution in managing corporate-divisional relationships.

Although this study has focused on the importance of the six factors enumerated above for maintaining effective relations between the headquarters and existing divisions, these determinants of effective conflict management should also be useful behavioral bench marks for companies which are faced with the problem of integrating newly acquired units. In this vein it is instructive to note that H-C Industries, which met the determinants to a higher degree, had enjoyed considerable success in integrating the companies it had purchased over the years. Indeed, H-C had never experienced a "post-merger slump" with a newly acquired unit. IPC, on the other hand, had experienced considerable difficulty in integrating several acquisitions which it had made in the late 1950's.

Having reviewed the major findings of this study, let us now turn to the question of how they relate to the problems of achieving synergy in highly diversified companies.

SYNERGY AND ORGANIZATIONAL PROBLEMS

Both Ansoff[11] and Kitching[12] suggest that synergy is not a homogeneous commodity. It appears that at least three major types of synergy can potentially be achieved in diversified firms. These are:

1. *Financial synergy*, which may be found in a large conglomerate's enhanced ability to obtain external funding and in its capacity to deploy capital internally to the most promising of a wide range of divisional ventures.
2. *Managerial synergy*, which entails the ability to develop and effectively apply both managerial talent and techniques to divisions, which if operating on their own, either could not afford or would not be motivated to secure such talent and techniques.
3. *Operating synergy*, which entails creating links among divisions either in terms of actual market and/or technical interdepen-

[11] H. Igor Ansoff, *Corporate Strategy* (New York: McGraw-Hill Book Co., 1965), chap. V.
[12] Kitching, *op. cit.*

dence (e.g., the flow of product) or in terms of the cross-pollination of marketing and technical skills.

The two firms in this study were heavily engaged in securing financial synergy. To a lesser degree they appeared to be achieving some managerial synergy—e.g., through the imposition of planning, budgeting, and funds requests systems and through limited interdivisional transfer of upper level managers. However, neither firm had achieved any significant results in terms of operating synergy. Why? H-C corporate management stated that it saw no immediate payoff from operating synergies because its divisions were simply too unrelated. Top management at IPC was actively interested in operating synergy but its attempts to nurture possible interdivisional collaboration had been relatively unsuccessful.

This state of affairs seems to fit with some other recent findings on the problems of achieving synergy. In a survey of 22 firms which had made 181 acquisitions, Kitching[13] found that

1. Concentric (broadly related) mergers had a considerably higher incidence of failure than conglomerate mergers.
2. Financial synergy was viewed as producing higher dollar payoffs and as easier to achieve than various types of operating synergy.

There appear to be at least two reasons why operating synergy is deemed less attractive as well as being fraught with considerable peril. First, it may entail coordinative costs that outweigh or greatly reduce the immediate—or even longer term—benefits it may provide. Certainly many diversifiers will require much more complex integrative systems than they currently tend to have if they plan to capitalize on operating synergy. This is one factor which seldom seems to be considered in premerger arithmetic.

The second reason why operating synergy tends to present problems may be that it is basically incompatible with the organizational arrangements which are now effective for achieving financial synergy. This study suggests that both appropriately high corporate-divisional differentiation and high integration are necessary for effective performance in highly diversified firms. Yet, headquarters emphasis on operating synergy may tend to inappropriately reduce corporate-divisional differentiation. In other words, the corporate office gets embroiled in the problems of achieving operating snyergy and in the

---

[13] *Ibid.*

process loses a good deal of the detachment and discipline that its role of evaluating division plans and allocating funds requires. How can you become heavily involved in divisional operations and still objectively evaluate them against competing alternatives? It seems entirely possible that, given the present organization of diversified firms, financial synergy and operating synergy are mutually antagonistic goals. This is not to say that operating synergy will ultimately be impossible or prohibitively expensive to achieve. The point is simply that different organizational arrangements from those which characterize the current research sites and many other conglomerates will be required to achieve operating synergy.

CONCLUSIONS

The comparative analysis of H-C and IPC suggests two broad conclusions about the effective management of highly diversified firms. These conclusions are:

1. *Overall corporate performance is related to there being a degree of corporate-divisional differentiation consistent with the product-market diversity faced by the firm and a degree of corporate-divisional integration consistent with the requirements of achieving control over total profitability and funds flow.*
2. *The joint decision-making process is both more efficient and more effective (a) when considerable weight is given to the requirements of both the corporate headquarters and the divisions and (b) when, consistent with adequate overall control, top management exhibits considerable flexibility in dealing with the diverse and changing demands posed by its divisions.*

One important assumption underlying this study and supported by its findings is that the managing system of a highly diversified firm is not a unitary function. Rather, it is a multi-level, joint decision-making activity in which (1) divisional managers identify and formulate plans for pursuing opportunities in particular industries and (2) corporate executives through their control of funds determine to which of these opportunities the firm as a whole shall direct its creative energies and productive resources. This may seem like an obvious statement, and yet most of the contemporary literature on business organizations either ignores the existence of joint decision-making or greatly belies its significance. In discussing the problems of managing conglomerates the current business press still steadfastly focuses on the activities of one or two men at the apex of the organizational pyramid. In his recent book, Professor John Kenneth Galbraith seems to err in the opposite direction by maintaining that corporate management, due to its minor participation in *substantive* decision-making, possesses only modest power in determining the direction of the industrial firm.[14] Reality appears to lie somewhere between these two extremes.

From the point of view of this study one of the critical organizational problems of a highly diversified firm is to maintain an active and high quality dialogue between the division managers who identify and formulate plans for capitalizing on opportunities and the corporate managers who decide whether these opportunities are ultimately to be pursued. The difficult task of corporate management, then, is to choose those divisional projects that best serve the overall goals of the corporation and still maintain an active generation of projects at the divisional level. This is what joint decision-making and integration are all about. Six factors have been identified which are important in maintaining this active and effective dialogue between corporate and divisional management systems.

While the most immediate utility of the findings reported in this chapter has to do with achieving integration, we should not ignore the important role that differentiation plays in managing the diversified firm. Rather than being an "organizational curse" which management must accept when it embarks on a diversification program, differentiation may well be a source of strength. If there is one characteristic of a highly diversified firm which makes it a unique and innovative organizational development, it is its ability to deploy capital and manpower across a wide range of areas of opportunity with considerably more flexibility than a large single-industry or vertically integrated firm. Much of this flexibility would seem to hinge on the ability of the corporate headquarters to maintain overall goals and orientations which are distinct from and not rooted in the particular industry identifications of its operating divisions. The implication is that top management should seek to maintain a high degree of corporate-divisional differentiation. At the same time, however, it appears that the patterns of differentiation and integration which are important for effectively making joint decisions around the issues of

---

[14] John K. Galbraith, *The New Industrial State* (Boston: Houghton Mifflin Co., 1967), pp. 69–71.

planning, budgeting, and resource allocation may be antagonistic to achieving operating synergy.

Although this study was designed to examine the particular organizational problems faced by highly diversified industrial enterprises, the problems of subunit diversity and joint decision-making around planning, budgeting, and resource allocation are common to all complex organizations—both in the public and private sectors of the economy. As these institutions face increasingly complex and changing conditions, explicit organizational planning becomes a critical skill; and thus knowledge concerning the options for and potential effects of organizational design and structural innovation also becomes increasingly important. The concepts of differentiation and integration provide a systematic analytical base from which administrators can identify these options and begin to gauge their behavioral effects.

3 | Organizational Choice: Product versus Function*

Arthur H. Walker and Jay W. Lorsch

This chapter considers one of the persistent organizational dilemmas facing managers—whether to structure the organization around products or by function. Using the concepts of differentiation and integration the authors provide a set of guidelines for considering this choice. They point to the fact that whichever pattern of formal organization is chosen, it can have an important impact on how people view their specialized tasks and on how they work together to achieve integration. The article which originally appeared in the *Harvard Business Review* is heavily based on Walker's thesis at the Harvard Business School. This research involved a comparative study of two manufacturing plants in the consumer food industry—one organized by function, the other by product. Walker is Associate Professor of Management at Northeastern University, while Lorsch is Associate Professor of Organizational Behavior at the Harvard Business School.

O F all the issues facing a manager as he thinks about the form of his organization, one of the thorniest is the question of whether to group activities primarily by product or by function. Should all specialists in a given function be grouped under a common boss, regardless of differences in products they are involved in, or should the various functional specialists working on a single product be grouped together under the same superior?

In talks with managers we have repeatedly heard them anguishing over this choice. For example, recently a divisional vice president of a major U.S. corporation was contemplating a major organizational change. After long study, he made this revealing observation to his subordinate managers:

* *Harvard Business Review*, November-December, 1968. © 1968 by the President and Fellows of Harvard College; all rights reserved.

"We still don't know which choice will be the best one. Should the research, engineering, marketing, and production people be grouped separately in departments for each function? Or would it be better to have them grouped together in product departments, each department dealing with a particular product group?

"We were organized by product up until a few years ago. Then we consolidated our organization into specialized functional departments, each dealing with all of our products. Now I'm wondering if we wouldn't be better off to divide our operations again into product units. Either way I can see advantages and disadvantages, trade-offs. What criteria should I use? How can we predict what the outcomes will be if we change?"

Companies that have made a choice often feel confident that they have resolved this dilemma. Consider the case of a large advertising agency that consolidated its copy, art, and television personnel into a "total creative department." Previously they had reported to group heads in their areas of specialization. In a memo to employees the company explained the move:

"Formation of the "total creative" department completely tears down the walls between art, copy, and television people. Behind this move is the realization that for best results all creative people, regardless of their particular specialty, must work together under the most intimate relationship as total advertising people, trying to solve creative problems together from start to finish.

"The new department will be broken into five groups reporting to the senior vice president and creative director, each under the direction of an associate creative director. Each group will be responsible for art, television, and copy in their accounts."

But our experience is that such reorganizations often are only temporary. The issues involved are so complex that many managements oscillate between these two choices or try to effect some compromise between them.

In this article we shall explore—from the viewpoint of the behavioral scientist—some of the criteria that have been used in the past to make these choices, and present ideas from recent studies that suggest more relevant criteria for making the decision. We hope to provide a way of thinking about these problems that will lead to the most sensible decisions for the accomplishment of organizational goals.

The dilemma of product versus function is by no means new; managers have been facing the same basic question for decades. As large corporations like Du Pont and General Motors grew, they found it necessary to divide their activities among product divisions.[1] Following World War II, as companies expanded their sales of existing products and added new products and businesses, many of them implemented a transition from functional organizations handling a number of different products to independently managed product divisions. These changes raised problems concerning divisionalization, decentralization, corporate staff activities, and the like.

As the product divisions grew and prospered, many companies extended the idea of product organization further down in their organizations under such labels as "the unit management concept." Today most of the attention is still being directed to these changes and innovations *within* product or market areas below the divisional level.

We are focusing therefore on these organizational issues at the middle and lower echelons of management, particularly on the crucial questions being faced by managers today within product divisions. The reader should note, however, that a discussion of these issues is immensely complicated by the fact that a choice at one level of the corporate structure affects the choices and criteria for choice at other levels. Nonetheless, the ideas we suggest in this article are directly relevant to organizational choice at any level.

ELEMENTS TO CONSIDER

To understand more fully the factors that make these issues so difficult, it is useful to review the criteria often relied on in making this decision. Typically, managers have used technical and economic criteria. They ask themselves, for instance, "Which choice will minimize payroll costs?" Or, "Which will best utilize equipment and specialists?" This approach not only makes real sense in the traditional logic of management, but it has strong support from the classical school of organization theorists. Luther Gulick, for example, used it in arguing for organization by function:

"It guarantees the maximum utilization of up-to-date technical skill and . . . makes it possible in each case to make use of the most effective divisions of work and specialization. . . . [It] makes possible also the economies of the maximum use of labor-saving machinery and mass production. . . . [It] encourages coordination in all of the technical and

---

[1] For a historical study of the organizational structure of U.S. corporations, see Alfred D. Chandler, Jr., *Strategy and Structure* (Cambridge, The M.I.T. Press, 1962).

skilled work of the enterprise. . . . [It] furnishes an excellent approach to the development of central coordination and control."[2]

In pointing to the advantages of the product basis of organization, two other classical theorists used the same approach:

"Product or product line is an important basis for departmentalizing, because it permits the maximum use of personal skills and specialized knowledge, facilitates the employment of specialized capital and makes easier a certain type of coordination."[3]

In sum, these writers on organization suggested that the manager should make the choice based on three criteria:

1. Which approach permits the maximum use of special technical knowledge?
2. Which provides the most efficient utilization of machinery and equipment?
3. Which provides the best hope of obtaining the required control and coordination?

There is nothing fundamentally wrong with these criteria as far as they go, and, of course, managers have been using them. But they fail to recognize the complex set of trade-offs involved in these decisions. As a consequence, managers make changes that produce unanticipated results and may even reduce the effectiveness of their organization. For example:

A major manufacturer of corrugated containers a few years ago shifted from a product basis to a functional basis. The rationale for the decision was that it would lead to improved control of production costs and efficiencies in production and marketing. While the organization did accomplish these aims, it found itself less able to obtain coordination among its local sales and production units. The functional specialists now reported to the top officers in charge of production and sales, and there was no mechanism for one person to coordinate their work below the level of division management. As a result, the company encountered numerous problems and unresolved conflicts among functions and later returned to the product form.

---

[2] Luther Gulick, "Notes on the Theory of Organization," in *Papers on the Science of Administration*, edited by Luther Gulick and Lyndall F. Urwick (New York, New York Institute of Public Adminstration, 1937), pp. 23–24.

[3] Harold D. Koontz and C. J. O'Donnell, *Principles of Management* (New York, McGraw-Hill Book Company, Inc., 2nd edition, 1959), p. 111.

This example pinpoints the major trade-off that the traditional criteria omit. Developing highly specialized functional units makes it difficult to achieve coordination or integration among these units. On the other hand, having product units as the basis for organization promotes collaboration between specialists, but the functional specialists feel less identification with functional goals.

Research Findings

We now turn to some new behavioral science approaches to designing organization structure. Recent studies[4] have highlighted three other important factors about specialization and coordination:

As we have suggested, the classical theorists saw specialization in terms of grouping similar activities, skills, or even equipment. They did not look at its psychological and social consequences. Recently, behavioral scientists (including the authors) have found that there is an important relationship between a unit's or individual's assigned activities and the unit members' patterns of thought and behavior. Functional specialists tend to develop patterns of behavior and thought that are in tune with the demands of their jobs and their prior training, and as a result these specialists (e.g., industrial engineers and production supervisors) have different ideas and orientation about what is important in getting the job done. This is called *differentiation*, which simply means the differences in behavior and thought patterns that develop among different specialists in relation to their respective tasks. Differentiation is necessary for functional specialists to perform their jobs effectively.

Differentiation is closely related to achievement of coordination, or what behavioral scientists call *integration*. This means collaboration between specialized units or individuals. Recent studies have demonstrated that there is an inverse relationship between differentiation and integration: the more two functional specialists (or their units) differ in their patterns of behavior and thought, the more difficult it is to bring about integration between them. Nevertheless, this research has indicated that achievement of both differentiation and integration is essential if organizations are to perform effectively.

---

[4] See Paul R. Lawrence and Jay W. Lorsch, *Organization and Environment* (Boston, Division of Research, Harvard Business School, 1967); and Eric J. Miller and A. K. Rice, *Systems of Organization* (London, Tavistock Publications, 1967).

While achievement of both differentiation and integration is possible, it can occur only when well-developed means of communication among specialists exist in the organization and when the specialists are effective in resolving the inevitable cross-functional conflicts.

These recent studies, then, point to certain related questions that managers must consider when they choose between a product or functional basis of organization:

1. How will the choice affect differentiation among specialists? Will it allow the necessary differences in viewpoint to develop so that specialized tasks can be performed effectively?

2. How does the decision affect the prospects of accomplishing integration? Will it lead, for instance, to greater differentiation, which will increase the problems of achieving integration?

3. How will the decision affect the ability of organization members to communicate with each other, resolve conflicts, and reach the necessary joint decisions?

There appears to be a connection between the appropriate extent of differentiation and integration and the organization's effectiveness in accomplishing its economic goals. What the appropriate pattern is depends on the nature of external factors—markets, technology, and so on—facing the organization, as well as the goals themselves. The question of how the organizational pattern will affect individual members is equally complex. Management must consider how much stress will be associated with a certain pattern and whether such stress should be a serious concern.

To explore in more detail the significance of modern approaches to organizational structuring, we shall describe one recent study conducted in two manufacturing plants—one organized by *product*, the other on a *functional* basis.[5]

PLANT F AND PLANT P

The two plants where this study was conducted were selected because they were closely matched in several ways. They were making the same product; their markets, technology, and even raw materials were identical. The parent companies were also similar: both were large, national corporations that developed, manufactured, and mar-

[5] Arthur H. Walker, *Behavioral Consequences of Contrasting Patterns of Organization* (Boston, Harvard Business School, unpublished doctoral dissertation, 1967).

keted many consumer products. In each case divisional and corporate headquarters were located more than 100 miles from the facilities studied. The plants were separated from other structures at the same site, where other company products were made.

Both plants had very similar management styles. They stressed their desire to foster employees' initiative and autonomy and placed great reliance on selection of well-qualified department heads. They also identified explicitly the same two objectives. The first was to formulate, package, and ship the products in minimum time at speci-

FIGURE 3.1

Organizational Chart at Plant F

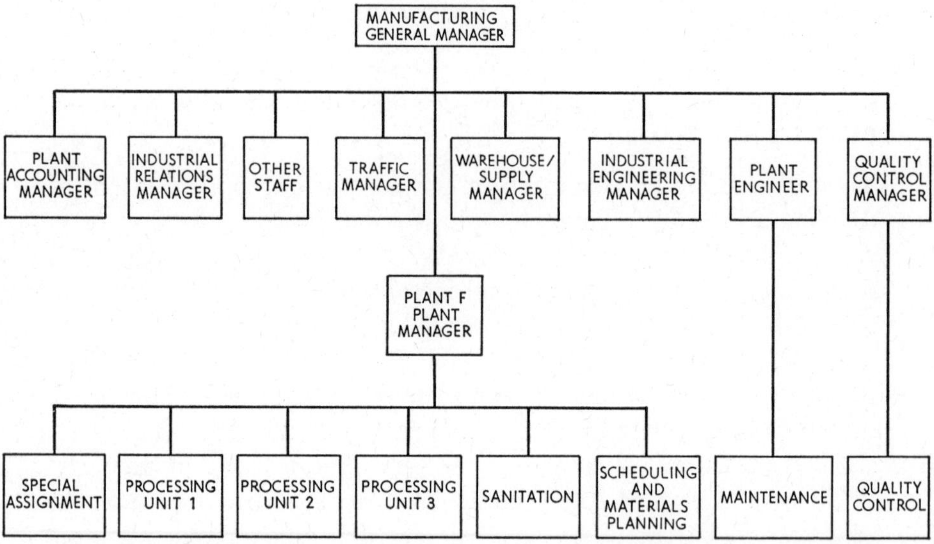

fied levels of quality and at minimum cost—that is, within existing capabilities. The second was to improve the capabilities of the plant.

In each plant there were identical functional specialists involved with the manufacturing units and packing unit, as well as quality control, planning and scheduling, warehousing, industrial engineering, and plant engineering. In Plant F (with the *functional* basis of organization), only the manufacturing departments and the planning and scheduling function reported to the plant manager responsible for the product (see Figure 3.1). All other functional specialists reported to the staff of the divisional manufacturing manager, who

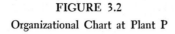

FIGURE 3.2

Organizational Chart at Plant P

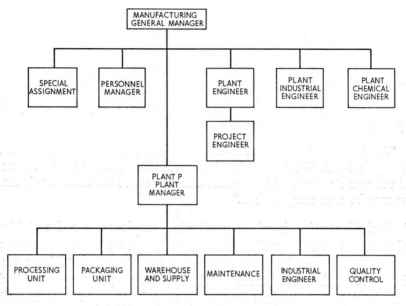

was also responsible for plants manufacturing other products. At Plant P (with the *product* basis of organization), all functional specialists with the exception of plant engineering reported to the plant manager (see Figure 3.2).

State of Differentiation

In studying differentiation, it is useful to focus on the functional specialists' differences in outlook in terms of:

Orientation toward goals.
Orientation toward time.
Perception of the formality of organization.

Goal Orientation. The bases of organization in the two plants had a marked effect on the specialists' differentiated goal orientations. In Plant F they focused sharply on their specialized goals and objectives. For example, quality control specialists were concerned almost exclusively with meeting quality standards, industrial engineers with methods improvements and cost reduction, and scheduling specialists with how to meet schedule requirements. An industrial engineer in Plant F indicated this intensive interest in his own activity:

"We have 150 projects worth close to a million dollars in annual savings. I guess I've completed some that save as much as $90,000 a year. Right now I'm working on cutting departmental costs. You need a hard shell in this work. No one likes to have his costs cut, but that is my job."

That these intense concerns with specialized objectives were expected is illustrated by the apologetic tone of a comment on production goals by an engineering supervisor at Plant F:

"At times we become too much involved in production. It causes a change in heart. We are interested in production, but not at the expense of our own standards of performance. If we get too much involved, then we may become compromised."

A final illustration is when production employees stood watching while members of the maintenance department worked to start a new production line, and a production supervisor remarked: "I hope that they get that line going soon. Right now, however, my hands are tied. Maintenance has the job. I can only wait. My people have to wait, too." This intense concern with one set of goals is analogous to a rifle shot; in a manner of speaking, each specialist took aim at one set of goals and fired at it. Moreover, the specialists identified closely with their counterparts in other plants and at divisional headquarters. As one engineer put it: "We carry the ball for them (the central office). We carry a project through and get it working right." At Plant P the functional specialists' goals were more diffuse—like buckshot. Each specialist was concerned not only with his own goals, but also with the operation of the entire plant. For example, in contrast to the Plant F production supervisor's attitude about maintenance, a Plant P maintenance manager said, under similar circumstances: "We're all interested in the same thing. If I can help, I'm willing. If I have a mechanical problem, there is no member of the operating department who wouldn't go out of his way to solve it."

Additional evidence of this more diffuse orientation toward goals is provided by comments such as these which came from Plant P engineers and managers:

"We are here for a reason—to run this place the best way we know how. There is no reluctance to be open and frank despite various backgrounds and ages."

"The changeovers tell the story. Everyone shows willingness to dig in. The whole plant turns out to do cleaning up."

Because the functional specialists at Plant F focused on their individual goals, they had relatively wide differences in goals and objectives. Plant P's structure, on the other hand, seemed to make functional specialists more aware of common product goals and reduced differences in goal orientation. Yet, as we shall see, this lesser differentiation did not hamper their performance.

Time Orientation. The two organizational bases had the opposite effect, however, on the time orientation of functional managers. At Plant F, the specialists shared a concern with short-term issues (mostly daily problems). The time orientation of specialists at Plant P was more differentiated. For example, its production managers concentrated on routine matters, while planning and industrial engineering focused on issues that needed solution within a week, and quality control specialists worried about even longer-term problems.

The reason is not difficult to find. Since Plant P's organization led its managers to identify with product goals, those who could contribute to the solution of longer-term problems became involved in these activities. In Plant F, where each unit focused on its own goals, there was more of a tendency to worry about getting daily progress. On the average, employees of Plant P reported devoting 30% of their time to daily problems, while at Plant F this figure was 49%. We shall have more to say shortly about how these factors influenced the results achieved in the two plants.

Organizational Formality. In the study, the formality of organizational structure in each functional activity was measured by three criteria:

1. Clarity of definition of job responsibilities.
2. Clarity of dividing lines between jobs.
3. Importance of rules and procedures.

It was found that at Plant F there were fewer differences among functional activities in the formality of organization structure than at Plant P. Plant F employees reported that a uniform degree of structure existed across functional specialties; job responsibilities were well defined, and the distinctions between jobs were clear. Similarly, rules and procedures were extensively relied on. At Plant P, on the other hand, substantial differences in the formality of organization existed.

TABLE 3.1

Differentiation in Plants F and P

Dimensions of Differentiation	Plant F	Plant P
Goal orientation	More differentiated and focused	Less differentiated and more diffuse
Time orientation	Less differentiated and shorter term	More differentiated and longer term
Formality of structure	Less differentiated, with more formality	More differentiated, with less formality

Plant engineers and industrial engineers, for example, were rather vague about their responsibilities and about the dividing line between their jobs and other jobs. Similarly, they reported relatively low reliance on rules and procedures. Production managers, on the other hand, noted that their jobs were well defined and that rules and procedures were more important to them.

The effects of these two bases of organization on differentiation along these three dimensions are summarized in Table 3.1. Overall, differentiation was greater between functional specialists at Plant P than at Plant F.

Integration Achieved

While the study found that both plants experienced some problems in accomplishing integration, these difficulties were more noticeable at Plant F. Collaboration between maintenance and production personnel and between production and scheduling was a problem there. In Plant P the only relationship where integration was unsatisfactory was that between production and quality control specialists. Thus Plant P seemed to be getting slightly better integration in spite of the greater differentiation among specialists in that organization. Since differentiation and integration are basically antagonistic, the only way managers at Plant P could get both was by being effective at communication and conflict resolution. They were better at this than were managers at Plant F.

Communication Patterns. In Plant P, communication among employees was more frequent, less formal, and more often of a face-to-face nature than was the case with Plant F personnel. One Plant P employee volunteered: "Communications are no problem around here. You can say it. You can get an answer."

Members of Plant F did not reflect such positive feelings. They were heard to say:

"Why didn't they tell me this was going to happen? Now they've shut down the line."

"When we get the information, it is usually too late to do any real planning. We just do our best."

The formal boundaries outlining positions that were more prevalent at Plant F appeared to act as a damper on communication. The encounters observed were often a succession of two-man conversations, even though more than two may have been involved in a problem. The telephone and written memoranda were more often employed than at Plant P, where spontaneous meetings involving several persons were frequent, usually in the cafeteria.

Dealing with Conflict. In both plants, *confrontation* of conflict was reported to be more typical than either the use of power to *force* one's own position or an attempt to *smooth* conflict by "agreeing to disagree." There was strong evidence, nevertheless, that in Plant P managers were coming to grips with conflicts more directly than in Plant F. Managers at Plant F reported that more conflicts were being smoothed over. They worried that issues were often not getting settled. As they put it:

"We have too many nice guys here."

"If you can't resolve an issue, you go to the plant manager. But we don't like to bother him often with small matters. We should be able to settle them ourselves. The trouble is we don't. So it dies."

Thus, by ignoring conflict in the hope it would go away, or by passing it to a higher level, managers at Plant F often tried to smooth over their differences. While use of the management hierarchy is one acceptable way to resolve conflict, so many disagreements at Plant F were pushed upstairs that the hierarchy became overloaded and could not handle all the problems facing it. So it responded by dealing with only the more immediate and pressing ones.

At Plant P the managers uniformly reported that they resolved conflicts themselves. There was no evidence that conflicts were being avoided or smoothed over. As one manager said: "We don't let problems wait very long. There's no sense to it. And besides, we get together frequently and have plenty of chances to discuss differences over a cup of coffee."

As this remark suggests, the quicker resolution of conflict was closely related to the open and informal communication pattern prevailing at Plant P. In spite of greater differentiation in time orientation and structure, then, Plant P managers were able to achieve more satisfactory integration because they could communicate and resolve conflict effectively.

Performance and Attitudes

Before drawing some conclusions from the study of these two plants, it is important to make two more relevant comparisons between them—their effectiveness in terms of the goals set for them and the attitudes of employees.

Plant Performance.   As we noted before, the managements of the two plants were aiming at the same two objectives:

1. Maximizing current output within existing capabilities.
2. Improving the capabilities of the plant.

Of the two facilities, Plant F met the first objective more effectively; it was achieving a higher production rate with greater efficiency and at less cost than was Plant P. In terms of the second objective, however, Plant P was clearly superior to Plant F; the former's productivity had increased by 23% from 1963 to 1966 compared with the latter's increment of only 3%. One key manager at Plant F commented:

There has been a three- or four-year effort to improve our capability. Our expectations have simply not been achieved. The improvement in performance is just not there. We are still where we were three years ago. But our targets for improvements are realistic.

By contrast, a key manager at Plant P observed: "Our crews have held steady, yet our volume is up. Our quality is consistently better, too." Another said: "We are continuing to look for and find ways to improve and consolidate jobs."

Employee Attitudes.   Here, too, the two organizations offer a contrast, but the contrast presents a paradoxical situation. Key personnel at Plant P appeared to be more deeply involved in their work than did managers at Plant F, and they admitted more often to feeling stress and pressure than did their opposite numbers at Plant F. But Plant F managers expressed more satisfaction with their work than did those at Plant P; they liked the company and their jobs more than did managers at Plant P.

Why Plant P managers felt more involved and had a higher level of stress, but were less satisfied than Plant F managers, can best be explained by linking these findings with the others we have reported.

Study Summary

The characteristics of these two organizations are summarized in Table 3.2. The nature of the organization at Plant F seemed to suit its stable but high rate of efficiency. Its specialists concentrated on their own goals and performed well, on the whole. The jobs were well defined and managers worked within procedures and rules. The managers were concerned primarily with short-term matters. They were not particularly effective in communicating with each other and in resolving conflict. But this was not very important to achieve steady, good performance, since the coordination necessary to meet this objective could be achieved through plans and procedures and through the manufacturing technology itself.

As long as top management did not exert much pressure to improve performance dramatically, the plant's managerial hierarchy was able to resolve the few conflicts arising from daily operations. And as

TABLE 3.2

Observed Characteristics of the Two Organizations

Characteristics	Plant F	Plant P
Differentiation	Less differentiation except in goal orientation	Greater differentiation in structure and time orientation
Integration	Somewhat less effective	More effective
Conflict management	Confrontation, but also "smoothing over" and avoidance; rather restricted communication pattern	Confrontation of conflict; open, face-to-face communication
Effectiveness	Efficient, stable production; but less successful in improving plant capabilities	Successful in improving plant capabilities, but less effective in stable production
Employee attitudes	Prevalent feeling of satisfaction, but less feeling of stress and involvement	Prevalent feeling of stress and involvement, but less satisfaction

long as the organization avoided extensive problem solving, a great deal of personal contact was not very important. It is not surprising therefore that the managers were satisfied and felt relatively little pressure. They attended strictly to their own duties, remained uninvolved, and got the job done. For them, this combination was satisfying. And higher management was pleased with the facility's production efficiency.

The atmosphere at Plant P, in contrast, was well suited to the goal of improving plant capabilities, which it did very well. There was less differentiation between goals, since the functional specialists to a degree shared the product goals. Obviously, one danger in this form of organization is the potential attraction of specialist managers to total goals to the extent that they lose sight of their particular goals and become less effective in their jobs. But this was not a serious problem at Plant P.

Moreover, there was considerable differentiation in time orientation and structure; some specialists worked at the routine and programmed tasks in operating the plant, while others concentrated on longer-term problems to improve manufacturing capability. The latter group was less constrained by formal procedures and job definitions, and this atmosphere was conducive to problem solving. The longer time orientation of some specialists, however, appeared to divert their attention from maintaining schedules and productivity. This was a contributing factor to Plant P's less effective current performance.

In spite of the higher degree of differentiation in these dimensions, Plant P managers were able to achieve the integration necessary to solve problems that hindered plant capability. Their shared goals and a common boss encouraged them to deal directly with each other and confront their conflicts. Given this pattern, it is not surprising that they felt very involved in their jobs. Also they were under stress because of their great involvement in their jobs. This stress could lead to dissatisfaction with their situation. Satisfaction for its own sake, however, may not be very important; there was no evidence of higher turnover of managers at Plant P.

Obviously, in comparing the performance of these two plants operating with similar technologies and in the same market, we might predict that, because of its greater ability to improve plant capabilities, Plant P eventually will reach a performance level at least as high as Plant F's. While this might occur in time, it should not obscure one important point: the functional organization seems to lead to better results in a situation where stable performance of a routine task is desired, while the product organization leads to better results in situations where the task is less predictable and requires innovative problem solving.

CLUES FOR MANAGERS

How can the manager concerned with the function versus product decision use these ideas to guide him in making the appropriate choice? The essential step is identifying the demands of the task confronting the organization.

Is it a routine, repetitive task? Is it one where integration can be achieved by plan and conflict managed through the hierarchy? This was the way the task was implicitly defined at Plant F. If this is the nature of the task, or, to put it another way, if management is satisfied with this definition of the task, then the functional organization is quite appropriate. While it allows less differentiation in time orientation and structure, it does encourage differentiation in goal orientation. This combination is important for specialists to work effectively in their jobs.

Perhaps even more important, the functional structure also seems to permit a degree of integration sufficient to get the organization's work done. Much of this can be accomplished through paper systems and through the hardware of the production line itself. Conflict that comes up can more safely be dealt with through the management hierarchy, since the difficulties of resolving conflict are less acute. This is so because the tasks provide less opportunity for conflict and because the specialists have less differentiated viewpoints to overcome. This form of organization is less psychologically demanding for the individuals involved.

On the other hand, if the task is of a problem-solving nature, or if management defines it this way, the product organization seems to be more appropriate. This is especially true where there is a need for tight integration among specialists. As illustrated at Plant P, the product organization form allows the greater differentiation in time orientation and structure that specialists need to attack problems. While encouraging identification with superordinate goals, this organizational form does allow enough differentiation in goals for specialists to make their contributions.

Even more important, to identify with product ends and have a common boss encourages employees to deal constructively with conflict, communicate directly and openly with each other, and confront their differences, so they can collaborate effectively. Greater stress and less satisfaction for the individual may be unavoidable, but it is a small price to pay for the involvement that accompanies it.

The manager's problem in choosing between product and functional forms is complicated by the fact that in each organization there are routine tasks and tasks requiring problem solving, jobs requiring little interdependence among specialists and jobs requiring a great deal. Faced with these mixtures, many companies have adopted various compromises between product and functional bases. They include (in ascending order of structural complexity):

1. *The Use of Cross-Functional Teams to Facilitate Integration.* These teams provide some opportunity for communication and conflict resolution and also a degree of the common identification with product goals that characterizes the product organization. At the same time, they retain the differentiation provided by the functional organization.

2. *The Appointment of Full-Time Integrators or Coordinators around a Product.* These product managers or project managers encourage the functional specialists to become committed to product goals and help resolve conflicts between them. The specialists still retain their primary identification with their functions.[6]

3. *The "Matrix" or Grid Organization, Which Combines the Product and Functional Forms by Overlaying Them.* Some managers wear functional hats and are involved in the day-to-day, more routine activities. Naturally, they identify with functional goals. Others, wearing product or project hats, identify with total product goals and are more involved in the problem-solving activity required to cope with long-range issues and to achieve cross-functional coordination.

These compromises are becoming popular because they enable companies to deal with multiple tasks simultaneously. But we do not propose them as a panacea, because they make sense only for those situations where the differentiation and integration required by the sum of all the tasks make a middle approach necessary. Further, the

---

[6] See Paul R. Lawrence and Jay W. Lorsch, "New Management Job: The Integrator," *Harvard Business Review*, November-December 1967, p. 142.

complexity of interpersonal plus organizational relationships in these forms and the ambiguity associated with them make them difficult to administer effectively and psychologically demanding on the persons involved.

In our view, the only solution to the product versus function dilemma lies in analysis of the multiple tasks that must be performed, the differences between specialists, the integration that must be achieved, and the mechanisms and behavior required to resolve conflict and arrive at these states of differentiation and integration. This analysis provides the best hope of making a correct product or function choice or of arriving at some appropriate compromise solution.

4 | Organizations in Two Cultures

André Ruedi and Paul R. Lawrence

This article reports an in-depth study of a German firm in the plastics industry. It was done so as to facilitate drawing comparisons with a set of six U.S. firms operating in the same highly technical and dynamic industry. The comparison serves to highlight the effect of culture on organization life and amply demonstrates the pervasive effect of cultural values and expectations. The study points to the aspects of the German culture that clash with the requisites for task in this industry and documents the organization's response to this performance. The implications of the study for management are rather self-evident—whether from the point of view of German managers, U.S. managers, or managers of multinational corporations. André Ruedi is currently a doctoral candidate at the Harvard Business School.

In his later work, the great anthropologist Bronislav Malinowski suggested that institutions would prove the ideal isolates for making comparisons between cultures. His contemporaries did not accept this suggestion because it seemed then that institutions were too large, with too many interdependent variables to be managed as units for cross-cultural studies. Further, there was some confusion about what institutions to compare. Malinowski defined institutions as social systems interacting in specific environments: "Institutions are groups attached to a certain part of the environment endowed with material equipment, the knowledge of how to use the equipment and the environment, linguistic usages enabling them to cooperate, roles and laws governing their behavior, and a body of beliefs and values shared in common." This paper reports on a study that has acted upon Malinowski's suggested approach and definitions of institutions.

We consider Malinowski's definition of institutions to be well within the conceptual framework of the open-systems approach to the study of organizations, and we resurrect Malinowski's suggestion at this time because the state of the art in organizational studies provides us with two tools that make his idea workable:

1. The multivariate approach, which reduces and quantifies the system variables to manageable proportions;
2. The contingency model of open-systems organizations, which permits us to stabilize the external variables and to select institutions which could fruitfully be used as isolates for cross-cultural comparisons.

The contingency model uses the concept of organizational effectiveness in various environments. Organizational effectiveness ultimately means the institution's ability to survive. By introducing a conditional judgment (Organization A is better in environments B and C than Organization Z), we seem to break the social scientist's tradition of value-free judgments in order to make a dynamic rather than a static comparison between two institutions and two cultures. Ultimately, all cultures compete with each other for survival over long periods of time. The concept of organizational effectiveness is therefore a dynamic tool. Further, the use of organizational effectiveness permits us to rank and select the more critical variables for comparison in some systematic way.

The institutions chosen for this comparative study were a German plastics company and six American plastics companies. The reasons for this are partly historic. The multivariate approach as used by Lawrence and Lorsch produced a considerable body of summarized and quantified data on American business organizations in three industries—containers, food, and plastics. Analysis of this data strongly confirmed the contingency model: different organizational forms and styles were most effective in different industries. We decided to do a cross-cultural study in the plastics industry because:

1. Six plastics organizations had been studied by Lawrence and Lorsch and only two food and two container companies, giving us better data in the plastics industry.
2. We found the plastics organizations to be more interesting as they evidenced a higher order of internal complexity and differentiation (in a biological analogy, the more highly differentiated organism is higher on the evolutionary scale).

Since the market and technology of the plastics industry is roughly the same in the United States and in Germany, organizational differences can be attributed largely to differences in culture. The characteristics of the plastics industry quoted below from Lawrence and Lorsch provide a feel for this environment and are relevant to the German as well as the U.S. setting.

For the sake of better comparability among organizations, we limited our study to firms that produced and sold plastics materials in the form of powder, pellets and sheets. Their products went to industrial customers of all sizes, from the large automobile, appliance, furniture, paint, textile and paper companies to the smaller firms making toys, containers and household items. The organizations studied emphasized specialty plastics tailored to specific uses rather than standardized commodity plastics. They all built their product development work on the science of polymer chemistry. Production was continuous with relatively few workers needed to monitor the automatic and semi-automatic equipment.

. . . [senior executives] indicated in interviews that the dominant competitive issue confronting them was the development of new and revised products and processes. The life cycle of products was dwindling. Without new products, any single firm was doomed to decline. And since all firms were steadily introducing new and revised products and processes, the future course of events was highly uncertain and difficult to predict.

According to these executives, the most hazardous aspect of the industrial environment revolved around the relevant scientific knowledge.

Comparative Economic Performance

Table 4.1 presents profitability data on leading German and U.S. chemical companies for a recent year. Such performance comparisons between U.S. and German firms can be somewhat misleading since the German numbers are probably deflated for tax purposes. Also the plastics segment of the chemical industry in which we are interested could present a somewhat different picture. Nonetheless, the numbers are supported by conversations with European and American industrialists who are unanimous in their opinion that U.S. competition is seizing an increasing share of the European plastics market from the native European companies and is achieving better profit margins.

Prior to World War II, cartels monopolized the plastics markets in Germany. Evidence of this approach to control of the market still remains with reputed agreements between German competitors to fix prices and exchange experimental products. In spite of such practices

TABLE 4.1

Large U.S. and German Chemical Companies
1966 Gross Sales and Profits*

Chemicals	Gross Sales ($B)	Profits as % of Sales
Du Pont	3.02	13.5
Union Carbide	2.06	11.0
Monsanto	1.47	8.4
Dow	1.18	9.2
Total	7.73	
Mean of 4 U.S. companies		11.2
Bayer	1.58	4.2
Hoechst	1.31	4.9
BASF	1.01	7.0
Total	3.90	
Mean of 3 German companies		5.1

* From Compagnie Lambert, quoted in the *American Challenge*, 1968.

and the traditional preference of German customers for established relationships with German firms, however, American companies were making heavy inroads. A German technical service manager stated:

[U.S. Co.] is able to beat us in our own market. They have the power and efficiency to beat us because, whereas we may have six technical service men in one area of the market, they'll have sixty. The other factor is that for some reason American plastics concerns seem to be able to produce more tons of material with less men than German industry can.

The German company chosen for this study, called Plastik AG, to disguise its real name, was, in 1967, one of the larger chemical firms in Germany, and one of the stronger economic performers among the German firms.

General Background on Plastik AG

Although Plastik AG was considered to be "progressive," it was definitely a German firm. As such, some general comments of Hartman's[1] on German industrial organizations are relevant and illuminating.

The organization of the [German] business firm is essentially a structure of authority relationships.

---

[1] Heinz Hartman, *Authority and Organization in German Management* (Princeton, N.J.: Princeton University Press, 1959).

Formal management structure of the typical German corporation consists of three separate groups: The supervisory board (Aufsichtsrat), The Executive Committee (Vorstand) and the members of upper management (Leitende Angestellte). The formal distribution of power clearly favors the Vorstand. The other two groups are considerably less powerful than their counterparts in other countries.

Each Vorstand member usually controls his own sector . . . This involves establishment of (several) hierarchies . . . each of which displays the characteristics of the more common single hierarchy in other firms.

This general picture held true for Plastik AG—its organization could be viewed as a nucleus of top managers (the Vorstand), each with an organization of his own which functioned as an extension of his person. Compared to the U.S. companies studied, the salient organizational factor in Plastik AG was its hierarchical information and decision structure. Decisions were made by people with the requisite formal authority—ultimately, the Vorstand. In most cases, the people who made the decisions were three or four levels removed from the people who had the detailed knowledge. This meant:

1. An elaborate formal vertical communications channel;
2. Limited time and short time horizon of key top managers;
3. Coordinating across functional departments done at very top levels.

The vertical communications network relied heavily on a formal letter writing and signing procedure. Plastik AG followed the standard German practice of limiting the right to sign letters (the Prokura) to senior middle management, although most of the detailed information was supplied by the lower echelons. Since the people who signed letters were responsible for the letter's contents, senior managers spent about one-third of their time reading letters prepared by people below them.

Of the 60 managers interviewed, the great majority sent more information up the hierarchy than they received from above. Data on the phenomenon is summarized in rounded form in Table 4.2.

The vertical communications system was strengthened by the code of hierarchical unity which worked to prevent informal lateral communications. "Don't show your dirty linen to others" and "present your best face to outsiders" were mottoes which describe the feelings that each department must show a united front to other departments.

TABLE 4.2

Volume of Information Processed up the Hierarchy
in Proportion to Volume Coming down

Level	Proportion of Information Processed up and down	No. of Respondents
Top...............1		2
2	2 times more up than down	4
3	4 times more up than down	10
4	5 times more up than down	16
5	8 times more up than down	20
6	10 times more up than down	8

Within a product group, formal integration among functional departments on non-routine matters, such as product modification, took place in high-level coordinating groups called the Kommission. There was a "lower" Kommission for each of the four major functional departments, chaired by the top man in that functional department (e.g., the sales Kommission was chaired by the director of plastics sales and a "main" Kommission chaired by a Vorstand member). All Kommissions were interdepartmental integrating bodies (but no research people were on the sales Kommission and no sales people on the research Kommission). The Kommission could delegate work to lower levels, but no interdepartmental work could be delegated by the Kommission. The Kommissions had permanent members (no proxy votes) and met every six to eight weeks. All decisions of the lower Kommissions had to be unanimous (each Kommission member had veto power). The climate of the Kommission system, as well as some of its underlying assumptions of leadership and authority, are well illustrated by the remarks of one high-level manager.

I can tell you that contrary to what you hear, the idea was primarily to get the responsible people together into a circle, a Kreis, for first, information exchange; secondly, coordination; and lastly, for making decisions. Decisions are not the main function of the Kommission. One might think so, because the members of the Kommissions have high status and have a lot of authority, but because they can make decisions in their positions does not mean that the Kommissions make a lot of decisions.

The conflicts at the (lower) Kommissions may involve 10 percent of the items on the agenda. At the main Kommission the conflict ratio is higher because you can't pass the buck upstairs. In general, I would agree that the higher you go, the more conflicts there are. And the final decisions are made at the very top. Each of the decisions made at the lower levels are conditional to approval from higher levels.

A Kommission can operate in two ways. It can make a decision first, and then ask for information from lower levels. Or it can ask for proposals from lower levels in order to make a decision. If a decision is made at the top first, it is much easier for the lower levels and produces no conflicts for them in any way. If, on the other hand, a decision is not made first, and information goes to the top for the purposes of making a decision, it produces conflicts on the way up.

The most important factor in a Kommission is the Kommission Chairman. He must know in advance how a decision must go. It is his responsibility to lead the Kommission to the right decisions. That is his duty.

Comparison of Differentiation and Integration Measures

In studying the German firm, we followed as nearly as possible the same methods used in the six U.S. plastics firms to measure the degree of differentiation. Measures were taken in each of the four basic units (sales, production, research and development, and technical service) in regard to three dimensions that were used in the U.S. study (degree of formality of structure, time orientation, and goal orientation).[2] The fourth dimension used in the U.S. study (interpersonal orientation) was omitted since the instrument was awkward to translate in a meaningful fashion and, more importantly, it was the least powerful dimension in the U.S. study in discriminating among basic departments. The findings on these three dimensions are summarized briefly below:

The average time orientation of the sampled German managers in the four basic departments was more similar to one another (less differentiated) than comparable managers in the high performing U.S. firms.

In terms of goal orientations, the German managers were more concerned with a diverse set of goals (less differentiated) in contrast to the more concentrated concern with departmental goals found among the managers of the high performing U.S. firms.

In regard to the third dimension, formality of structure, all four departments of the German firm were remarkably alike. They all made extensive use of formal rules. They all set up quite specific standards for reviewing both departmental performance and the performance of individual managers. They all tended to review performance at relatively short intervals.

---

[2] See Lawrence and Lorsch, *Organization and Environment* (Boston: Division of Research, Harvard Business School, 1967).

This was in contrast with the high performing U.S. firms where there were especially sharp differences between the low degree of formality of structure in research and the high degree in production departments.[3]

The overall scores on interdepartmental differentiation as well as integration are given in Table 4.3. It is striking that the total differentiation score of the German firm is markedly less than the lowest scoring firm in our U.S. sample of six. The evidence is clear that the German firm was in some way constraining its major departments from adopting a structure and orientation that would make a good fit with their respective environmental and task characteristics. There apparently existed a press for conformity that was interfering with the

TABLE 4.3

Scores for Interdepartmental Differentiation (Three Dimensions) Integration, and Relative Performance for 1 German and 6 U.S. Plastics Companies

	Interdepartmental Differentiation	Interdepartmental Integration	Relative Economic Performance
U.S..........1	7.5 (High)	5.7 (High)	High
2	7.3 (High)	5.6 (High)	High
3	6.3 (Low)	5.3 (High)	Medium
4	6.8 (High)	5.1 (Low)	Medium
5	7.0 (High)	4.9 (Low)	Low
6	5.0 (Low)	4.7 (Low)	Low
German.....	3.8 (Low)	5.1 (Low)	

type of high differentiation that was associated in this industry with high performance in the U.S. firms.

In studying the German firm, we used the same scale employed in the United States to measure the quality of interdepartmental integration. In the U.S. study, this measure was strongly associated with our measures of overall performance. Table 4.3 also presents our findings on this factor. It can be seen that the German firm is again low on this score compared to the U.S. firms. This is true even though the researchers saw several indications that the integration scores were

---

[3] In talking to managers from the research and production departments in the German firm, we got the distinct impression that the research department was even more formally structured than production. There seemed to be tighter control and more detailed supervision. We were not in a position to delve into all the reasons behind this apparent reversal of the expected pattern but it might be partially explained by the fact that the research laboratories were centrally located while many of the production units were geographically dispersed.

somewhat biased on the high side due to the German code of presenting internal unity to an outsider. The instrument used to establish differentiation was more indirect and therefore less open to such bias.

The combination of a low integration score with a very low differentiation score clearly indicates that the German firm had not developed the kind of internal characteristics that were associated with high performance in the U.S. companies. These results go a long way to explain why the German firm was a low performer relative to the U.S. firms even though it performed well by German standards.

We will explore below some additional data about this firm that suggests some of the reasons behind these findings. In particular, we will review the same factors found in the U.S. studies that helped account for the quality of differentiation and integration achieved. All are concerned with the conflict resolution or decision making process.

Comparison of Conflict Resolution Factors

Integrative Devices. In the U.S. study, an examination was made of the various kinds of structural methods used to facilitate integration in addition to the universally used methods of a managerial hierarchy and a paper control system. It was found that all six companies used roughly the same additional devices. Specifically, they had all established ground rules that permitted and even encouraged managers at all levels to make direct contact with other managers anywhere in the system with whom they had some interdependency. In addition, they had all set up some relatively permanent teams or committees concerned with product planning and decision making whose memberships represented all the basic functional areas. These cross-functional teams were usually on at least two different levels of the structure. Finally, all the U.S. firms had established a major department whose primary function was to facilitate integration between the other three basic departments.

When we looked for comparable mechanisms in the German firm, we found some revealing differences. First, a ground rule existed about direct managerial contacts across departmental lines that was clearly more restrictive than that customary in the U.S. firms. One of the German executives, in speaking of crossing departmental lines, explained the company norms:

You certainly cannot go to a higher level in another department. That would be impossible. You can go to people at your own level. But the problem is that they prefer to deal with people in their own department. The second problem is that I don't even know who has the information I need.

As we indicated in the earlier description of the German firm, they had established "Kommissions" that were roughly the counterpart of the U.S. cross-functional teams. However, the Kommissions existed only at the level in the German firm that roughly corresponded to the highest of the several levels at which we found these teams in U.S. firms. In other words, the crossover coordination was occurring at a higher level than in the U.S. companies.

Finally, the German firms' department of development and technical service (DTS) was positioned between the sales, production, and research departments so that in some ways it was a counterpart of the integrative departments in the U.S. firms. It was significant, however, that its charter did not specify integration as a major function. This fact is revealing in the light of Burns's findings that such offices do a better job of integrating when it is clearly perceived that integration is their major function.[4] In summary, the same formal structural devices to facilitate conflict resolution which were present in the U.S. firm were found in the German firm, but they were clearly affected by the German predilection for upper level decision making and following the hierarchy.

Intermediate Position of Integrative Department.   In the U.S. plastics firms an association was found between the quality of integration achieved and the degree to which the integrating department was structured and oriented in ways that were intermediate in respect to the departments' whole work they were expected to integrate.[5] As a point of comparison, we examined the orientations of the managers of the DTS department in the German firm for this characteristic. We found that the DTS managers did, on the average, hold time and goal orientations that were intermediate in respect to the basic departments. There is, therefore, no reason to think that this factor was impeding the achievement of integration.

Influence of Integrators Derived from Technical Competence.   An additional difference between U.S. firms that achieved high integration and those with low integration was whether managers who held integrating roles were deriving their influence more from their perceived competence or from their formal positional authority. The

---

[4] See James Burns, "Effective Management of Programs," Chapter 8 of this text.
[5] Lawrence and Lorsch, *op. cit.*, pp. 58–62.

former condition seemed to contribute to better integration. As we interviewed managers in the German firm, we noted that the vast majority of managers who commented on the matter saw the DTS managers as deriving their authority from their position rather than from their competence. A few of the typical comments about DTS are given below.

The attitude of DTS was not cooperation—it was just control.

*   *   *   *

There are some people in DTS who are very good. They have good contact with the market and product applications. . . . However, the top-heavy structure of DTS prevents us from dealing directly with those people who would be most helpful.

*   *   *   *

These and other comments suggest that the research and sales managers felt that the decisions were made at the higher levels in DTS by people without detailed knowledge. The more junior managers at DTS were often respected for their technical competence but these men seem to have had only limited influence.

Rewards of Integrators Related to Total Systems Performance. In the U.S. study it was found that a relationship existed between the quality of integration and the extent to which integrators felt rewarded for overall results. While we were not able to measure this factor in the German firm in a systematic manner, our interviews indicated what DTS personnel perceived to be the basis of reward:

We (DTS) are too conservative and too influential. We don't want to introduce a completely new product, even a much improved product, to the market. There's too much risk involved for us.

*   *   *   *

Every man tries to cover himself in his job description and will not attempt any work that is not specified in his domain.

*   *   *   *

I think all of my colleagues are as careful as I am because if something goes wrong, it would be very bad for all of us. Therefore, we'd rather play it safe, take a little longer, spend a little more.

These and similar quotes reveal a mixed perception about what is rewarded—avoiding mistakes, following proper channels, sticking to one's defined job—but none of these people mention achievement of the overall task of effective product innovation. Apparently, these concerns were reserved for only a very few top managers.

High Influence throughout the Organization.   In the U.S. plastics firm a relationship was found between effective conflict resolution and an overall perception by managers at all levels that they personally have relatively high influence on decisions. The two U.S. companies enjoying the best integration record each scored 3.6 on this measure, while the two lowest rated companies in integration were at 2.6 and 3.1 on the measure. The German firm scored 3.8. Thus, the German firm scored higher on this factor than any of the U.S. companies. This quality taken by itself could be expected to facilitate integration. The fact that in a number of interviews managers spoke of their lack of a sense of personal influence throws some doubt on our questionnaire results, but we have no way of further checking their validity. The sample quote below indicates some of the contra evidence.

In my position as a [junior manager], my influence is zero. In fact, any [junior manager's] influence is zero. The situation is that I have trained for a long time—seven years—to make a doctorate in chemistry. I do not feel that the work that I do now uses even a fraction of my abilities. It's a waste—a laboratory technician could do the work that I am doing.

Influence at Requisite Level.   In the earlier study of the plastics industry, it was ascertained, given the environmental circumstances each basic department needed to relate, that the knowledge needed to make sound decisions in regard to product innovation tended to be concentrated at different echelons in each department. A higher level production manager could best be expected to have the knowledge to consider interdepartmental decisions. For sales, it was more likely that managers in the middle of the hierarchy would have the relevant knowledge. In both research and the integrating department, managers in the lower ranks tended to have the more detailed knowledge critical to effective product innovation decisions. When these requisites were compared with the actual distribution of influence by levels in each of these departments in the U.S. firms there was an association between having the locus of influence at the required level and effective conflict resolution. The firm with the most effective integration had the highest influence at the requisite level in four out of four departments. The next three most effectively integrated companies had the influence at the requisite level in three out of four departments. The two least well integrated organizations had the highest influence at the requisite level in two out of four departments. By comparison, the German firm had the highest influence at the requisite level in two (production and DTS) of the four basic departments. In both the sales and research departments, however, the actual influence was concentrated at a higher level than was predicted as requisite for effective integration. This finding was strongly supported by such comments as those below:

Another problem is that the real technical talent and the experience in dealing with particular products resides at a comparatively low level. But these people do not get to see our products. Our products go to the upper levels where people are over-worked and do not have the fine feel for the product and the market.

*   *   *   *

The problem gets aggravated when our bosses make decisions about technical matters when they don't have the technical information to make these decisions. Then we are faced with a decision that has been made which we feel is wrong. That's maddening.

*   *   *   *

Even though we found consistent testimony on the existence and importance of this problem, one manager indicated that the situation was worse in other German firms.

We have relatively much more authority at low levels than other German firms. This is due first to the nature of the industry and secondly to our top man in production who consciously delegates to his subordinates as much as he can—more than in the other plastics firms.

Modes of Conflict Resolution. The final factor that was systematically studied in the U.S. plastics firms in regard to conflict resolution had to do with the predominant mode or style of conflict resolution that was employed throughout the firm. Three styles of resolution were identified: confrontation—the process of sharing relevant facts and opinions and struggling through the disagreements in a problem-solving way; forcing—the use of authority or power to settle conflicts by overruling dissent; and smoothing—the handling of conflict by minimizing differences, postponement, or superficial compromise. It was found that the firms achieving more effective integration made more extensive use of confrontation with only a secondary use of forcing.

We were not able to use a comparable questionnaire in the German firm that would permit us to quantify this factor. However, we did elicit a considerable number of comments on the style of conflict resolution used. As nearly as we could tell from this data, smoothing or avoidance was the predominate way of handling conflict in the lower and middle levels of management. At the higher level, some mixture of forcing and confrontation seemed to be used, with an especially heavy use of forcing.

Below is a small sample of the quotations from which these conclusions were derived.

My comment is that the higher the position of the members, the more personal the fighting gets in the meetings. One gets the impression, listening to them, that the feeling for an objective solution is lost—and that they try to blame each other or place each other in a bad light. The resolution of these conflicts, these power conflicts is by forcing through or by political maneuver and compromise.

*   *   *   *

The decisions in the Kommission are made by simple majorities. There are often strong disagreements.

*   *   *   *

[In reference to decisions taken on middle levels] Somebody calls all the people together and they have a discussion. We can get a resolution much easier in a small group because you can get into details and bring in a [junior manager]. At these meetings, then, a compromise is usually reached.

We have reviewed the evidence on seven different factors that, according to the earlier study in U.S. firms, had a bearing on the fact that the German firm was experiencing considerable difficulty in achieving effective integration as well as differentiation. Our review of these seven factors reveals why. While two of the factors were seen to be facilitating integration, the other five were not. In particular, the researchers judged that the fact that many decisions were made at levels above where the needed knowledge existed was especially damaging to the integrative process. The other factor that also seemed to be especially salient was the heavy use of forcing and smoothing rather than confrontation as the customary style of resolution of conflict.

We have now completed a review of Plastik AG's organizational characteristics compared to U.S. firms in the same industry in terms of (1) degree of differentiation between major departments, (2) the quality of integration existing between major departments, and (3) the set of factors influencing the conflict resolution process between departments. The differences are indeed striking. The German firm scores extremely low on measures of differentiation and in this regard it is clearly deviant from the requirements of the dynamic and diverse environment of the plastics industry. Its integration quality is also low and we saw above the separate factors that especially seemed to contribute to this condition even though differentiation was low. These findings dramatically pose the question of why this German firm, clearly one of the leaders in resources, talent, and results among German chemical firms, should be operating in a way that is demonstrably so far out of line with the requirements of its market and technical environment. At the start of this article the authors expressed an interest in the way culture influences organizational patterns. We will now address this source of influence more directly and in detail. Can the influence of the German culture account for the differentiation and integration findings?

German Cultural Factors

Much culturally learned behavior was thought to be biologically instinctive until comparison with another culture's behavior pattern showed otherwise. Culture has been defined as the social heredity of a society. One element of culture is the behavior code that through early training becomes so deeply imbedded in the individual that it forms part of his unconscious reaction to situations. Cultural training also includes a unique language and a system of values. The value system provides a view of self in relation to the society, a view of the world at large, and concepts of correct behavior within the society and vis-à-vis the physical environment. Linguists have shown that language not only serves as a vehicle for communication but that, in addition, each language systematically categorizes phenomena into classes of experience in a different way. Thus language directly and strongly influences the way an individual interprets his perceptions and the way he thinks. Each culture, therefore, provides its members with a three-element set: behavior code; value system; and language.

As stated before, we will restrict our comparison of German and U.S. cultures to specific institutions (and even there we can only scratch the surface), but before going into this specialized setting we will summarize the cultural differences in the wider society as provided by some of the general literature on the subject.

One valuable study that highlights the differences in cultural values is a 10-year old comparative study of German and U.S. high

FIGURE 4.1

Differences in the Values, Motives and Activities of German and
American High School Boys Aged 16–19*

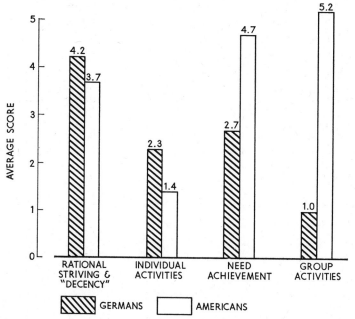

* Differences between the two countries are highly significant in each comparison. (After
McClelland *et al.*)

school boys.[6] Figure 4.1 presents some critical data from this study
and the excerpts below clarify their general meaning.

Cultures may be conceived as working out various patterned solutions
to the double obligation to the individual and society. In the U.S., a high
spontaneous interest in achievement is counter-balanced by much experience in group activities in which the individual (implicitly) learns to
channel his achievement according to the opinions of others.

In Germany the reverse is true. The pattern starts with an explicit
recognition of ones obligations to work hard and to live up to an idealistic
code of decency governing interpersonal behavior. The matrix of mutual
obligations is clear and is consciously taught and learned. If there is a
problem for Germans it is in the area of maintaining individuality in the
light of such strong social obligations. They solve it by insisting on the
importance of power over oneself . . . not by achieving in uniformity

---

[6] D.C. McClelland, J. F. Starr, R. H. Knapp, and H. W. Wendt, "Obligations to
Self and Society in the U.S. and Germany," *Journal of Abnormal and Social Psy-
chology*, Vol. 56 (1958), as quoted in McClelland, *Roots of Consciousness* (Princeton,
N.J.: D. Van Nostrand Co., Inc., 1964).

with group expectations as in the U.S. but by proudly controlling selfish interests to fulfill explicit duties to the whole society. The sense of self comes not from achievement but from self-direction and control.

The insistence on a rational systematically worked out code which governs the system of interpersonal obligations produces the famous German success at devising orderly and efficient organizations. Max Weber's conception of a bureaucracy as an institution governed by universalistic rules—applicable to everyone—is a good example of this kind of thinking. And German bureaucracies—including particularly the civil service are efficient, orderly, and highly admired by the Germans themselves. An army as a special type of bureaucracy also thrives under such a value formula. A modern army requires orderliness and rational chains of command and above all discipline. Hehce, it is not surprising that Germans make good soldiers and have produced excellent armies. They have the values that armies need.

Researchers have theorized that the achievement motive or need for achievement referred to in Figure 4.1 is composed of two elements: the positive need to approach success and the negative need to avoid failure.[7] Americans' need for achievement is about two-thirds positive and one-third negative. The German researcher Heinz Heckhausen has published several papers using hope for success and fear of failure as subcategories in need for achievement, and has reported a strong fear of failure component in Germans, estimated at one-half the total need for achievement drive.[8]

We have summarized only two of the available studies of German culture but other studies also tend to show that the Germans have a view of self, work, superiors, organizations, career, etc., that is different from those of the Americans. These views directly affect and limit the total organizational possibilities. Let us recapitulate; Germans in comparison with Americans have:

Stronger fears of failure and of displeasing superiors;
Stronger desire for explicit and stable relationships, structures, and methods;

---

[7] J.W. Atkinson, and G. H. Litwin, "Achievement Motive and Test Anxiety Conceived as Motive to Approach Success and Motive to Avoid Failure," *Journal of Abnormal and Social Psychology*, Vol. 60 (1960).

[8] Heckhausen, H., *Hoffnung und Furcht in der Leistungsmotivation* (Meisenheim/Glan: Hain, 1963); "Ueber die Zweckmaessigkeit einiger Situationsbedingungen bei der inhaltsanalytischen Erfassing der Motivation," *Psychologische Forschung* 27 (1964), 244–59; "Leistungsmotivation," in *Handbuch der Psychologie*, Bd. 2. (Goettingen: Hogrefe, 1965); mit Kemmler, Lilly und Meyer, Wulf-Uwe, "Validierungskorrelate der Inhaltsanalytisch Erfassten Leistungsmotivation Guter und Schwacher Schueler des Dritten Schuljahres," *Psychologische Forschung* 28, 1965.

Stronger attraction to individual as against group activities;
Greater tendency to idealize reality; and
Lower Need Achievement drive.

These general tendencies are interwoven with the many institutions of German life and manifest themselves as organizational characteristics. The strong authoritarian relationship with the father, for instance, is transferred to a strong subordinate-superior role set in the university (where a Ph.D. candidate spends an average of seven years as a particular professor's assistant) and to a similar subordinate-superior role set in German business. This role set is quite explicit and manifests itself as a "proper" sense of duty and loyalty to the superior.

Cultural Factors at Plastik AG

These cultural factors proved to be in evidence at Plastik AG, as was shown by our clinical interview data and data from several questionnaire instruments administered to our sample of 60 managers.

In this regard, we administered a four-picture thematic apperception test (TAT) which was scored for need for achievement, need for power, and need for affiliation. We see that the numbers in Table 4.4 strongly support the general data. Need for achievement in Plastik AG was extremely low compared to the high performance U.S. company. The German's need for power is higher and their need for affiliation lower. Note that there was a wider difference in need for achievement scores between Plastik and U.S. managers than between the McClelland German/American high school sample.

But the TAT offers us more. For instance, a picture of two well-dressed men, one older and the other younger, talking face to face at arms length inside a well-appointed office, brought out two radically different themes from the German and American respondents. Both

TABLE 4.4

Need Achievement, Need Power and Need Affiliation for
60 German Managers in Plastik AG compared to 70 U.S.
Managers in High Performing Firm*

	Plastik AG	U.S. Company†
Need achievement................1.25		4.0
Need power.....................6.7		5.9
Need affiliation.................2.1		3.3

* Higher number indicated greater need.
† U.S. figures adjusted for four-picture TAT.

groups tended to identify with the younger man. For the Americans, the prevalent theme was that the younger man is the boss of an older subordinate whose work is in danger of becoming marginal. The most prevalent German theme, however, had the older man as the boss or father admonishing his subordinate-son for straying from the true path. This was a recurrent German theme: the young man attempts

FIGURE 4.2

Profile Sheet for the Organizational Climate Questionnaire
(Revised Form A)*

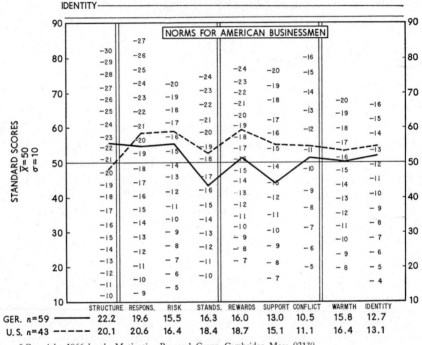

	STRUCTURE	RESPONS.	RISK	STANDS.	REWARDS	SUPPORT	CONFLICT	WARMTH	IDENTITY
GER. n=59 ———	22.2	19.6	15.5	16.3	16.0	13.0	10.5	15.8	12.7
U.S. n=43 - - - - -	20.1	20.6	16.4	18.4	18.7	15.1	11.1	16.4	13.1

* Copyright, 1966, by the Motivation Research Group, Cambridge, Mass. 02139.

individuality by trying new methods or a nonapproved career, and is confronted by the superior-father. The young man almost inevitably bows to authority and gives in.

We begin to see that the wider culture establishes some parameters for the organization operating within the culture. To translate the cultural traits of the organization's membership into some dimensions used in describing business organizations, we used a 50-item organizational climate questionnaire which describes the organization on 9 dimensions.[9] Figure 4.2 shows these dimensions for Plastik AG and for the high performing U.S. company.

Although there is no significant difference on any one dimension, there is a consistent picture. The Germans reported more structure and less of everything else. Also interesting is the fact that the Germans reported higher responsibility and risk than the U.S. norm.

The following are some interview excerpts which illustrate the German's fear of failure and fear of his boss. A Ph.D. production supervisor:

My relationships with my boss are very good, because I used to be his assistant when he had my job, and I know how he used to work. And he did many of the same things that I do that are not really supposed to be done. I can make small changes in the process without formally consulting him or anyone. Then if it works, I'll tell him. If not, I'll cover the error by mixing the material with some other material—and nothing is said.

A Ph.D. production supervisor:

My boss has a very strong opinion and he's very hard; if he gets angry he yells at you, and he's likely to throw something at you. It becomes difficult to disagree with him. You could disagree with him, but you certainly couldn't convince him. Even if an experiment proved him wrong and me right, there would be small victory because it would never be mentioned again. He certainly would not say, "Well, you were right and I was wrong." If we disagree, and I do what I think is right and it doesn't work, I'm in trouble. If we disagree, and I do what I think is right, and it works—he gets the credit.

A Ph.D. group leader in DTS:

We don't have to fear our bosses. At least I don't have to fear my boss. Those days really are over for us in Germany. But, on the other hand, you still try to keep your boss quiet. It does depend on who your boss is. There are those bosses who could inspire fear.

A Ph.D. section leader in research: "My boss and I have such good contact that we speak openly about all our problems. . . ." At this point during the interview with this manager, the phone rang. He ignored the phone for a while. The secretary came in and said: "There's a phone call . . ." He interrupted with, "I do not want to be

---

[9] Developed by G. H. Litwin, 1966. See G. H. Litwin and R. Stringer, *Motivation and Organizational Climate* (Boston: Division of Research, Harvard Business School, 1969) for a description of this instrument.

disturbed." She said, "Yes, but it's the secretary of [a Vorstand member]." "Aha, I'll take it," he said. On the phone he said, "Yes, Mr. Gama. Yes, Mr. Gama. Yes, Mr. Gama," and so on during the entire conversation. The impression this observer had was that Dr. X seemed quite rigid and frozen in an uncomfortable position. After the phone call, he said, in a much more relaxed tone, "That was Mr. Gama. I see him twice a week in routine talks, and he was just following up something."

The evidence is abundant that the general features of the German culture did show up in the internal features of Plastik AG. These particular cultural traits foster the adoption of a set of organization practices that can help in the performance of tasks with certain kinds of technical and market environments, but not the kind of environments found in the plastics industry. The Plastik AG organization can be thought of as in a press between two inconsistent forces, task requirements and cultural expectations.

While gathering evidence about the existence of this conflict, the researchers were also observant of indications about its dynamics— how was the pressure being handled? We will address this question in the next section.

Dynamics of Task-Cultural Conflict

Given the differentiation and integration configuration at Plastik AG and the press between task and cultural requirements, we would expect to find some people sticking to the cultural influences and thereby creating delays and blocking the innovation process. On the other hand, we would expect to find the pressures for task accomplishment to result in some organizational accommodations. The evidence in this regard is illuminating.

In the earlier U.S. research it was found that the most critical competitive issue in the plastics industry generally was a firm's competence in regard to new product innovations. As we would expect from its low rating in both differentiation and integration, Plastik AG was experiencing difficulty in this aspect of the business. Not only did the relatively high structure and shorter term orientation of the research group seem to diminish creativity, but the problems of moving potentially competitive new product ideas through DTS to production and sales was especially frustrating.

Lack of Innovation. The following comments illustrate that lack of innovation of new products was one of the more serious problems facing Plastik AG (as well as other German companies).

A sales engineer:

The tendency is clear. Germany had in the pre-war era some great chemical researchers—not any more. Today the competition keeps coming up with new products and we have to work very hard just to stay abreast. We inform DTS and there the information gets divided into many technical groups and chopped up like an onion. The machine starts grinding and comes out with many reasons why the product can't be done. Only when the Vorstand gets involved is there any hope that we will come up with a competitive product.

A Ph.D. chemist in production who spent three years in research: "There is very little sympathy in this company for new products or processes."

A Ph.D. chemist in production who spent one year in research: "From our point of view, you could leave research out of the organization and it wouldn't change the picture at all. They haven't produced anything new in five years."

Ph.D. chemist in research: "I want to make clear that the work we do here is just copying work. We do not do any kind of productive research in the larger sense. We just copy the competition. We are not producing new products."

Even when product ideas were judged to be valuable, delays in moving the idea forward caused frustrations.

A group leader in research: "Our department is very good. We are extremely efficient but we are not utilized because of the bureaucratic and very slow reaction of DTS."

A DTS group leader: "Oh, the mail! It takes five minutes to write a letter but it takes fourteen days to get it out of the house."

A production engineer:

It takes too long to decide something because you need too damn many signatures of people sitting at desks who don't really know what it's all about. And either they're not there and the letter waits on their desk or they don't know and you have to inform them; or they're picayune and find small faults and send it back for corrections. The whole process takes too much time.

A research chemist:

When we transfer a product to DTS, who are neutrals, they just work on it on a routine basis. They will not look for what is not written on the ticket which accompanies the product. You should see that lab. You can't blame them, they are terribly overworked. There is no room for initiative in processing our products. If it doesn't meet the narrowly specified criteria, they don't look for any other uses that this product could have. The results take three months to get back from DTS.

These delays had a detrimental effect on the organization's ability to react rapidly to market changes. A DTS man who had worked in the United States stated that in the United States new products come out faster, not because they are better qualified but because contacts between departments are clear and less complex.

The strong vertical communication and decision structure placed great demands on top management's time for the solution of short-run problems. Consequently, many longer range problems were delegated to staff functions. Further, the limited time available to superiors contributed strongly to the inadequate downward communications, as the following quotes indicate.

The director of plastics sales: "You must understand that my boss is on the Vorstand and consequently I see him very seldom."

A Ph.D. in research: "We do not have enough information to work optimally. The information resides at upper levels but the flow is blocked by the time constraints of our supervisors. They don't have enough time to inform us. That doesn't mean that they don't try— they try, but they don't have the time."

A director of development of DTS: "I spend about 40% of my time reading mail and distributing it to the lower section with appropriate comments."

Plastik AG's difficulties in regard to innovation and rapid response were, as we have seen, fairly widely recognized in the company. People were finding a variety of ways of responding to these problems. The trouble was, however, as we shall see, many of these responses only compounded the problem.

Organization Responses

A number of people were responding to the difficulties they were experiencing by leaving the firm. Exact figures are not available but several managers confided that Plastik AG lost half its new hires within six months. An internal study circulated to middle managers reported that half of those leaving would have been valuable to the company and suggested a more tolerant attitude towards new subordinates.

One young manager said: "It's the ambitious people that tend to leave. Many young people, and in my opinion some of the best, leave within six months. In spite of this high turnover, we are still more modern than other German companies."

Another response to the rigidity of the organization was a tendency for each major department to duplicate within its own boundaries the functions of the other major departments. Thus, for example, there was a product applications group in sales, paralleling the function of the product applications group in DTS; a burgeoning physical testing group in research paralleling that in DTS; a market research group in DTS paralleling the function of market research in sales; and a polymerization effort in DTS paralleling that function in research. Some of the managers explained how this redundancy came about.

A middle level manager:

Officially it is all very beautiful and smooth. But behind the scenes you have a constant conflict between groups and a constant repetition of the basic pattern of duplicating other groups' functions in your own department.

A salesman:

Because of the friction between DTS and sales, the plastics sales department decided to form its own new technically staffed applications group within the sales department. DTS is very big and slow to respond. By having our own applications group we can exert leverage against DTS to get work done.

A chemist in research:

The physical testing group in DTS presents a bottleneck. Even though we have a formal stamp with a big rush on it we can't get it back fast enough. We are starting now to do some of our own physical testing and perhaps the solution is to have our own physical testing group here in research.

A DTS chemist:

Everyone tends to build up his own domain at the expense of someone else. These competitive overlaps occur almost spontaneously and are tolerated by the top because this phenomenon has had a long history in our organization. . . . There is a great discrepancy between the formal way in which coordination between departments is supposed to occur and the way it really happens. Formally, the function and boundaries of groups are clear and relations between groups are good. Unfortunately, there is much competition because each group wants to increase its own power. This feeling increases secrecy and distrust between departments.

These comments document the apparently spontaneous occurrence of structural redundancy in the absence of low-level cross-functional integration. These redundancies were closely related to the additional response of overstaffing. As noted before, Plastik AG (like other European plastics companies) uses more manpower to produce a ton of plastics than U.S. companies. Although this is partly explained by economies of scale, there are other factors at play: empire building to get ahead and the fact that unwieldy communications nets and decision structures often require the same work to be done several times.

A DTS group leader noted: "Now I have a small group. I don't have the power to sign letters, but it's a question of time. These DTS groups will really grow after we get to a certain size. They'll have to give me the letter-signing power."

A production engineer: "Your personal career progress in this company depends upon the number of people you have under you, so everyone is trying to get as many people working for him as he can. Each man tries to build his empire."

The various responses discussed above are interdependent and reenforce each other. Some of the responses we see were motivated by a sincere desire to get the job done in spite of the organization, but the net result was questionable from the standpoint of overall effectiveness. In addition, we saw some signs of change that were the beginnings of more fundamental alterations in the prevailing pattern. For example, the following interview excerpt is from a DTS executive who had spent several years working in the United States:

I can tell you the normal way to make interdepartmental contacts, but I'm taking the short cuts more and more and I think more people are taking the short cuts because it works when we do it. . . . But you take a risk every time you do it. It might happen for instance that you forget to inform somebody important. Then you are not covered in case you are not successful. The normal chain of command you have short-cutted gets very upset that they haven't been informed; they feel threatened. The average employee who is afraid of his position would not take the short cut. Not more than 5% of DTS employees take short cuts. I have been very lucky. I have taken chances that might have gone wrong, but none of them did.

This interview was unique in presenting an attitude of risk-taking within a concept of man-made and changeable organization. There were indications that there sometimes were unusually high rewards for those who at great personal risks successfully managed to "beat the system."

The pressure for improved lateral communications was also evidenced by the increased use of Telex and the telephone instead of writing.

A Ph.D. chemist in DTS:

My boss has a pile of letters a foot high on his desk and it takes him two weeks to clear it. I cut through all of that whenever I can by phoning the client directly. But there are many problems that can't be answered by phone. I'll tell you a little secret. We do have another short cut. We use the Telex. I can sign a Telex without any other approval (a Telex signature is not legally binding, a signed letter is). There is no selectivity in what goes by Telex, except what is possible to answer by Telex. This does not mean that the less important problems go by Telex and the more important by mail—not at all! I supposed this could give rise to a serious problem because my boss is no longer automatically informed, but luckily this hasn't happened yet.

These comments indicate that the hierarchical information system was not changing through a conscious plan but was being changed through pressure of work and new technology at its weakest points.

Besides the above examples of personal risk-taking and informal changes in the information net, we saw another approach to changing the system. That is a new (for Germany) personal work style that some younger managers were attempting to establish in their own groups.

A sales manager:

I am very proud of my section. I think I have the best people working for me. This section runs itself. Everyone says to me "you're so lucky, you have the best people." I have the best people because I develop the best people. I am not a stickler for letters and things of that sort. If someone writes a letter, I'll just sign it—once he knows how. Some of the other managers will read each letter very carefully, ponder over a word, take out a pen, cross out the word and say "No, I don't think this word will do." Then the whole letter has to be written again. This kind of thing discourages people. When I'm not here, my people make decisions in my absence. And then they tell me, "in your absence I made this decision." I'll say "that's fine." You should see how they glow when I say that.

A group leader in research: "We work as a team. I was exposed to American laboratory organization through our exchange program. I am trying to introduce the team concept here."

A group leader in research: "There are many young people coming in, many of whom have been in the States and their attitudes to working cooperatively will provide a new climate here—and we badly need it."

These signs of fundamental change were relatively few and from the authors' point of view, it is regrettable that they were labeled as "American" rather than simply a style of management that better fit the requirements of this particular kind of task.

Summary and Conclusions

In *The American Challenge*,[10] a recent best seller in Europe, the Frenchman, J. J. Servan-Schreiber, argues that Americans are increasingly dominating the European industries with a high technological content and that the technological gap between Europe and America is widening:

Most striking of all is the strategic character of American industrial penetration. One by one, U.S. corporations capture those sectors of the economy most technologically advanced, more adaptable to change, and with the highest growth rates.

The greater the degree of technological advancement [measurement by the number of scientists and engineers as percentage of total number of employees], the greater the American role.

At the last meeting, in Paris, of the Atlantic Pact, the subject that dominated the debates was this technological gap. It is the major problem of our time; but I believe that the technological gap is misnamed. It is not so much a technological gap as it is a managerial gap. And the brain drain occurs not merely because they have more advanced technology in the United States but rather because they have more modern and effective management.

Europe's lag seems to concern *methods of organization* above all. The Americans know how to work in our countries better than we do ourselves.

For Servan-Schreiber the solution is primarily a political one—to make the ruling classes change the educational system to conform to the demands of contemporary management methods. Our analysis

---

[10] J. J. Servan-Schreiber, *The American Challenge* (New York: Atheneum Publishers, 1968).

shows the problem to be deeper rooted in the culture itself. The composite picture drawn from the six U.S. plastic companies shows that in this industry effective organization requires a style that is "foreign" to most of our German samples. Our look at Plastik AG has given us ample evidence that it is an organization under strain due to two opposing pressures: (1) the traditional and culturally ingrained view of organizations as authority structures, requiring explicit, stable and strong hierarchical relationships with "ultimate" authority at the top; and (2) the task-related pressure to integrate information across functional lines at levels where the detailed information resides—and to make decisions as close as possible to these levels.

A group leader at DTS: "The organization here is set up on military lines. But for new products, military organizations are not the most efficient. What we need, in military parlance, is a commando unit with the power to break through and act as a product team. But we can't do this because it would cross other people's territory and alliances. The primary loyalty of most people is their boss and setting product teams would fuzzy this relationship."

A product supervisor: "I spent three months working in the States. So I know something about the American system. I saw it. And I know it well enough to make some comparisons. We couldn't just go over to the American system of teamwork. Our people are used to working alone."

These comments illustrate that there is an awareness of a problem, that the pressures are making themselves felt, but that change is seen as difficult. Our culture data has shown that explicit vertical relationships and working alone are part of the German cultural set. These factors are deeply ingrained and part of a viable cultural system, which has become institutionalized in German life. The need for clear vertical relationships, for instance, is deeply related to feelings of dependence and need for stability, as the following comment illustrates.

A group leader in research:

I think we should have more structure in the Research Department. Even if we lose some flexibility in moving people from job to job. I personally would like to have the formal authority that goes along with the responsibility that I carry out in my function. Right now, if something goes wrong, it would be better if I had the formal authority than if I don't. Imagine if there is something that goes wrong, if there is a mistake. There has to be someone responsible who gets the blame.

We can perceive that the cultural value sets of "normal" Germans would tend to interfere with their assuming more flexible roles in low level product teams. In essence, effective team members would be cultural deviants. An edict from on high could not turn a culturally adjusted person into a cultural deviant. Hiring cultural deviants for these tasks could be a solution, but it is difficult to imagine an institution long established in the culture consciously giving positions of power to cultural deviants.[11]

The press between culture and task can be clearly perceived around the issue of size. The interview with a Vorstand member cited earlier shows that one of the recognized problems in competing with U.S. firms is the smaller size of German firms. This produces disadvantages in the scale of production, capital investment, and research. Yet there were strong indications that Plastik AG, given its present style, was nearing a size limit.

A section leader in research made a typical comment:

Our main problem, as I see it, organizationally is that we are too big. [Der ganse Laden ist zu gross]. We should go to division management, like they do in the States. There is too much power concentrated at the very top. Of course, there are drawbacks to decentralization. But, in the long run, these are offset by the advantages.

But, like establishing low-level integration, setting up divisional management would intrude into the cultural set. And the people at the top of the system are the least likely to encourage a diminution of their authority. After all, they have paid their dues for getting to the top. For them, there are strong "rational" reasons to keep the system going.

A Vorstand member said:

As compared with us, I find the management of Dow or Dupont very clumsy and ill-formed. They are so decentralized into divisions that if you want to make an agreement with them, the men at the top don't have the information at their fingertips. It takes them months to develop a viewpoint, whereas we have the information and authority to make an agreement on the spot.

Not only is the present organization supported at the top, but by a large number at all other levels as this quote by a group leader in DTS illustrates:

---

[11] Yet this is exactly what U.S. firms seem to be doing in hiring "atypical" Germans to work for them in Germany.

I would like to make a comment on the difference between the U.S. system and the German one. As I see it, the major difference is that in Germany you don't get switched out of your job. I think our system is better even at the cost of carrying some zeros in positions of power. A firm of this size can certainly afford its share of zeros. I know that the company will take care of me, even if someday I become calcified. Germany provides a better climate for individuals than does America. The Americans are too concerned about money. I have a sense of freedom that stems from the security I have in this job.

These quotes indicate the basis for our expectation that the conflict between the task requisites and the cultural set will continue.

Our research has shown that there is a contingent relation between culture, the nature of tasks, and task effectiveness. The logical implications are that given conditions of a free world market, nations will either have to specialize in industries whose technological complexity "fits" their culturally determined approach to organization or they will have to change their culture. The only other logical alternative would be to step back to trade restrictions and the formation of cartels which protect less-efficient industry.

To our knowledge, cultures have very seldom changed consciously from the top down. There is considerable evidence that the German (and European) culture is changing—being influenced by American values. But this change proceeds slowly, by generational spurts. Whether this change will be large and fast enough is open to question. What does appear to be happening—according to Servan-Schreiber—is the first alternative: an international division of labor—splitting the world economy roughly into three zones: a first zone of a highly developed technological society responsible for discoveries and innovation; a second zone, mainly Europe, whose role it would be to produce the discoveries made elsewhere; finally, a third zone of underdeveloped nations to provide raw materials and simple industrial products using traditional methods. Whether this approximate division of labor will persist is difficult to predict. This one research has thrown additional light on some of the fundamental causes of this phenomenon and some factors that would be involved in changing it.

5 | Organizational Characteristics and Individual Motivation

John J. Morse

Morse examines the connection between individual motivation and organization in this paper which, although preliminary, may have far-reaching implications. His basic finding is that when a functional unit has formal organizational practices and a climate which fit the requirements of its particular task, the unit will be effective and the members of the unit will be more motivated. It is the latter point which is novel and intriguing, for it suggests that designing and developing an organization to fit the demands of its environment may also provide important psychological rewards for the members of the organization. The chapter reports on Morse's doctoral thesis at the Harvard Business School. Morse, who is an assistant professor at the Graduate School of Business Administration at the University of California at Los Angeles, is currently working on an extension of this study with Professor Lorsch.

IN designing an organization and any functional unit within managers must decide which organizational characteristics will get the job done with the people available to do the work. Managers have been helped by a number of recent studies that focus on the relationship of organizational design and task performance. For example, Burns and Stalker give some clues to the kind of organizational design that makes sense for the effective performance of a highly structured or a highly unstructured task: they label these two patterns of organizational characteristics "mechanistic" and "organic" respectively.[1] And Argyris, among others, looks at organizational patterns that appear to be useful primarily in unstructured task settings, although

---

[1] Tom Burns and G. M. Stalker, *The Management of Innovation* (London: Tavistock Publications, 1961).

his major concern seems to be providing for the needs and wants of individuals in the organization.[2] However, managers have been pretty much let down in terms of studies that try to link organizational characteristics in both structured and unstructured task settings to the motivation of the individuals who do the work in them. Just as important, there is little behavioral science data available that simultaneously link organizational characteristics with both effective task performance and individual motivation. Not so surprisingly, even the well-informed manager adopts the attitude that it may be possible to build an organization to get the task done well, or to build an organization to satisfy the needs of the people in it, but that the accomplishment of either one of these two goals may require a compromise in the other.

In the field of organizational theory and practice and in the field of motivational psychology, there seem to be some ideas that could possibly begin to fill in these gaps. In the first place, the proposal of a "contingency model" of organizations made sense in terms of achieving effective task performance.[3] According to the model, an organization's characteristics or attributes should be appropriate to, or should "fit," the kind of task being done. There is no one best way to organize in all task situations: rather, a manager should analyze his task in terms of (1) its degree of predictiveness, routineness, or certainty, and (2) its dominant concern or its major competitive issue. The manager should then design his organization to reflect these dimensions of the task in order to achieve high task performance. For example, a successful manufacturing plant doing the relatively routine and certain job of turning out standardized household appliances would probably have organizational attributes that differed markedly from those of a successful research laboratory working on basic chemical research.

Some questions occurred to us after an examination of this model. When an organization pattern fits the task requirements of the task organization, what led to effective performance or behavior on the part of the individuals in the organization and, therefore, to effective performance for the organization as a whole? More specifically, could fit situations, by engaging and fulfilling certain kinds of needs

---

[2] Chris Argyris, *Integrating the Individual and the Organization* (New York: John Wiley & Sons, Inc., 1964).

[3] See Paul R. Lawrence and Jay W. Lorsch, *Organization and Environment* (Boston: Division of Research, Harvard Business School, 1967).

and wants, motivate the managers and professionals in such settings to successful task performance? An especially useful approach to answering that specific question came from the area of motivational psychology. Here, an individual is viewed as having an active tendency or need to master and tame his external environment, including the task environment that he faces when he chooses to become a member of a particular work organization.[4] The accumulated feelings of satisfaction that come from successfully meeting and mastering an environment are called a "sense of competence." We felt that this "sense of competence" could possibly help explain how fit setting could motivate individuals toward high and successful performance. The reasoning was that an organizational fit situation motivates individuals precisely because it leads to a sense of competence from mastering a particular task environment. Another way of putting this is to say that the kind of behavior that results when organizational characteristics are appropriate to the task is the kind of behavior that leads to effective task performance, and that the individual is motivated to perform such behavior because it leads to his experiencing feelings of mastery and competence.

In summary, then, because of some gaps in the current knowledge concerning organizations and their functioning, we wanted to see if we could link organizational characteristics of both structured and unstructured tasks to individual motivation and, second, if we could point out the impact of that first link on task performance so as to tie organizational design simultaneously to both individual needs and task accomplishment. When we speak of organizational characteristics here, we speak in general in terms of their degree of appropriateness to the task according to the contingency model. And, when we speak of individual motivation here, we mean an individual's sense of competence from mastering a particular task environment.

The Research Study

The study that was subsequently designed focused on measuring the feelings of competence or the sense of competence in four functional task units, two each in two very different kinds of task

---

[4] See Robert W. White, "Ego and Reality in Psychoanalytic Theory," *Psychological Issues*, Vol. III, No. 3, New York: International Universities Press, 1963.

environments.[5, 6] These environments posed two very different kinds of tasks and, therefore, from the contingency model, called for very different kinds of organizational characteristics for successful perform- ance. One environment was dealing with a highly routine, predictable and certain task, producing standardized containers manufactured on high-speed, automated production lines. The other was dealing with a highly unpredictable, uncertain, rapidly changing task, com- munications technology research and development. Two large compa- nies were approached, one with a number of similar containers manu- facturing plants and one with a number of similar communications research laboratories. In both cases, top company executives were asked to select one unit that they judged to be a highly effective performer and one that they judged to be a less-successful or low performer. It was expected that such differences in performance would be preliminary clues to the differences in fit, which would allow us to test our ideas about the links between organizational characteristics, individual motivation, and task performance. Our study sites looked like this:

	Certain Manufacturing Task	Uncertain Research Task
High performer, as initial clue to high de- gree of "fit"	Akron containers plant	Stockton communications research laboratory
Less successful performer, as initial clue to lower degree of "fit"	Hartford contain- ers plant	Carmel communications research laboratory

Dimensions of Fit

For all four of the functional units studied, that is, for both the high and low performer in both the certain and uncertain task envi-

---

[5] John J. Morse, "Internal Organizational Patterning and Sense of Competence Motivation" (unpublished doctoral dissertation, Harvard Business School, Boston, 1969).

[6] We should point out that, while the "contingency model" deals with both the differentiation, or task specialization, between functional task units such as manu- facturing, sales and research departments and then the integration of those units into a unity of effort, we in our study decided it was wiser to focus only on the notion of differentiation in the model and correspondingly to deal only with functional task units such as manufacturing plants and research laboratories. We felt that it was in such units that the individual ultimately confronted his task environment and that it was there that the organizational characteristics might have their most potent influence on his motivation to perform effectively.

ronment, it was necessary to define what was meant by "fit," or to define what kinds of organizational attributes or characteristics to look at to gauge how appropriate the unit's organizational design was to its particular task. "Fit" as used in this study was made up of two things. First, it was "formal fit," or fit between the kind of task being done and the formal practices that the unit used to get its job done. And, formal practices meant:

1. The pattern of formal relationships and duties, as signified by organization charts, position descriptions, procedural manuals, etc., and whether or not this pattern approached a high or low degree of structure;
2. The pattern of formal rules, formal operating and control procedures, formal standards and measurements, etc., and again whether or not this pattern approached a high or low degree of structure;
3. The time dimensions incorporated in the formal practices above, and if those practices stressed a long- or short-term time frame; and,
4. The goal dimensions incorporated in the formal practices, and if those practices stressed manufacturing, sales or scientific goals.

Second, fit was "climate fit," or fit between the kind of task being worked on and the perceptions and orientations that had developed among the individuals in the functional unit. "Climate" is really the aspect of the organizational setting that is subjectively perceived or experienced by the individuals in the unit.[7] In this study "climate" signified:

1. The structural orientation in the unit, that is, whether or not individuals in the unit perceived their behavior to be tightly controlled and structured;
2. The time orientation in the unit, that is, whether individuals were more concerned with the long- or the short-term;
3. The goal orientation in the unit, that is, whether individuals were more concerned with manufacturing, sales or scientific goals;
4. The distribution of influence in the unit, that is, how much total influence was perceived in the unit and whether the distribution of that influence was perceived to be concentrated in the upper levels of the formal structure (hierarchical distribution) or more evenly

---

[7] See Renato Tagiuri and George H. Litwin (ed.), *Organizational Climate: Exploration of a Concept* (Boston: Division of Research, Harvard Business School, 1968).

spread out among more levels in the formal structure (egalitarian distribution);

5. The top executive's "managerial style," that is, whether individuals in the unit perceived their chief executive to be more concerned with the task and getting the work done or more concerned with people and establishing and maintaining good interpersonal relations;

6. The character of superior-subordinate relations in the unit, that is, how much "say" individuals in the unit perceived they had with their superiors in choosing the kind of task they were to work on and in doing the task on their own once it had been chosen; also, the perceptions of the type of supervision in the unit, if it was seen as being more directive or more participatory; and,

7. The character of colleague relations in the unit, that is, the perceptions of how similar colleagues were in backgrounds, education, prior work experiences, strategies for tackling job-related problems, etc., and the perceptions of the degree of coordination of effort or the unity of effort among colleagues in the unit.

We asked a cross section of about 30 managers and professionals in each of our study sites to take short tests that measured all the attributes listed above in order to determine the degree of fit between the organizational characteristics and the kind of task being worked on. We then used our measurement of the feelings of competence of the managers and professionals in the units to investigate our ideas on the link between fit and sense of competence motivation.

The Major Findings of the Study

To point up the principal findings of the study, we will compare and contrast the data collected in the high performer in the certain task environment (Akron containers manufacturing plant) with the data collected in the high performer in the uncertain environment (Stockton communications research laboratory). However, it is necessary first to recognize an important aspect of this research. Because Akron and Stockton performed tasks at the opposite ends of the spectrum of certainty and tasks with different dominant concerns, we anticipated that there would have to be major differences between them on the organizational characteristics of fit if they were to perform effectively. So, as we point out the differences in these attributes of organizational design as we found them in the two high performing units, we will also be pointing out differences that we had expected and predicted using a contingency model approach.

Differences in the Characteristics of "Formal Fit" in Akron and Stockton

The Akron and Stockton organizations fit their respective tasks better than did their less-successful counterparts in Hartford and Carmel. In the certain task environment in which Akron operated, the pattern of formal relationships and duties was highly structured and precisely defined, while in Stockton in the uncertain task environment, that pattern had a low degree of structure and was much less precisely defined. We also found that Akron's pattern of formal rules, procedures, control sytsems, etc., was pervasive, specific, uniform and comprehensive. One manager in Akron went so far as to say: "Good God! We've got rules here for everything from how much powder to use in cleaning the toilet bowls to how to cart a dead body out of the plant." In contrast, Stockton's formal rules were minimal, loose and flexible. One scientist there, when asked if he felt the rules ought to be tightened, said: "Hell, no. We produce and we produce under relaxed conditions here. Why tamper with success?"

Akron's highly structured formal practices were appropriate to its certain task because behavior there had to be rigidly defined and controlled around the automated production line. There was really only one way to accomplish Akron's very routine and programmable job, and managers there defined that way precisely and insisted that each man in the plant do what was expected of him in order to achieve the high coordination of effort that was necessary to get the job done well. On the other hand, Stockton's highly unstructured formal practices made just as much sense because behavior there simply could not be rigidly defined. In such an unpredictable, fast-changing field as communications technology research, there was more than one way to get the job done well and Stockton's managers therefore said they could not define any one and only way. They correspondingly used an unstructured pattern of formal practices that left scientists in the laboratory free to behave as the changing task situation required.

Akron's formal practices were also very much geared to short-term manufacturing concerns. For example, formal reports and review sessions were daily occurrences, consistent with the fact that the throughput time was typically a few hours for the kind of containers manufactured.

By contrast, Stockton's formal practices were geared to long-term scientific concerns. For example, formal reports and reviews ordinarily occurred only quarterly, semiannually or annually. This was appropriate because research at Stockton often did not come to fruition for three to five years.

These differences in the characteristics of "formal fit" in the two high performers are summarized in Table 5.1. The two less-effective sites, the Hartford containers plant and the Carmel research laboratory, had formal organizational characteristics that were not as appropriate for their respective tasks. For example, Hartford's formal prac-

TABLE 5.1
Differences in the Characteristics of Formal Fit in Akron and Stockton

	Akron (Certain Manufacturing Task)	Stockton (Uncertain Research Task)
1. Pattern of formal relationships and duties	Highly structured, precisely defined	Low degree of structure, less well defined
2. Pattern of formal rules, procedures, controls, measurements, etc.	Pervasive, specific, uniform, comprehensive	Minimal, loose, flexible
3. Time dimensions incorporated in formal practices	Short-term	Long-term
4. Goal dimensions incorporated in formal practices	Manufacturing	Scientific

tices were much less structured and controlling than Akron's, while Carmel's were more restraining and restricting than Stockton's. It would not be too far off base to say that the organizational characteristics of formal fit in the less-successful Carmel research laboratory approached those in the high-performing Akron manufacturing plant, and that the formal practices in the low-performing Hartford plant were similar to those in the highly effective Stockton research laboratory.

Differences in the Characteristics of "Climate Fit" in Akron and Stockton

Concerning the differences in the characteristics of "climate fit," our findings in general showed that Akron and Stockton again fit their tasks better than Hartford and Carmel did. In the more certain manufacturing task environment, Akron's managers perceived a great deal of structure in their plant, and they were highly oriented toward the short-term and toward manufacturing goals. In contrast, Stockton's professionals perceived very little structure in their laboratory and they were highly oriented toward the long-term and toward scientific goals. Appropriately, perceptions of high structure and of precisely defined behavior were just what Akron needed to ensure that each man was conforming to the uniform set of behavioral prescriptions that the automated production flow demanded. One manager said: "We can't let the lines run unattended. We lose money when they do. So we make sure each man *knows* his job, *knows* when we can take breaks, *knows* how to handle a change in shifts, etc. It's spelled out for him the day he comes to work here." And, Akron's managers said that their orientations to short-term manufacturing goals meant that they tended to seek quick feedback from customers concerning the quality and service that the plant was providing—this kind of behavior is certainly conducive to high performance in this kind of environment. In Stockton, though, the perceptions of less structure sanctioned the relaxed, individualistic, and creative behavior that the uncertain, rapidly changing research task called for. Likewise, Stockton's researchers said that their orientations to long-term scientific goals meant that they were willing to rely on long-term feedback from a research project that might take years to complete. One scientist said:

"We're not the kind of people here who need a pat on the back every day. We can wait for months if necessary before we get feedback from colleagues and the profession. I've been working on one project for three months now and I'm still not sure where it's going to take me. I can live with that, though."

This is the kind of behavior and attitude that tends to spell success in this kind of environment.

We also found that Akron and Stockton differed substantially on their distribution of influence and on the character of superior-subordinate and colleague relations. With the certain task, Akron's managers perceived much less total influence in their plant than Stockton's professionals did with their uncertain task. In Akron, individuals felt that their task did not require continual reworking or reformulation: the task in Akron had already been well defined and there was less need there than in Stockton's continually changing task for individuals to have a say in decisions concerning the work process. Also, in Akron, influence was perceived to be concentrated in the upper levels of the formal structure (a "top-heavy" distribution), while in Stockton influence was perceived to be more evenly spread out among more of the levels in the formal structure (egalitarian distribution). Akron's managers felt they had a low degree of freedom with their superiors both to choose the tasks they were to work on and to handle the task on their own once it had been chosen. They also described the type of supervision in the plant as being relatively directive. Stockton's scientists, on the other hand, felt they had a great deal of freedom with their superiors both in the choosing and execution of tasks or projects. They also described the type of supervision in the laboratory as being very participatory. Concerning colleague relations, Akron's managers perceived a great deal of similarity among themselves in backgrounds, prior work experiences, and approaches for solving job-related problems. They also perceived the degree of coordination of effort among colleagues to be very high. Stockton's researchers perceived a great deal of differences among themselves and perceived the coordination of effort or the unity of effort among colleagues to be relatively low.

Akron's top-heavy distribution of influence and directive type of supervision meant that decision-making tended to be concentrated at the top levels in the organization. This made sense in this certain environment because the information necessary to make the critical decisions, especially decisions concerning overall scheduling of the plant, resided at the top. In fact, we attended one scheduling meeting in Akron where the plant manager informed his managers that there had been a change in the top management of one of their best customers. He said that he had decided on the basis of this information, information that no one else in the plant could as easily have had, ". . . to flood him with containers so that he'll get the message quickly that we're the best supplier he has available to him." With the requisite knowledge to make decisions at the top, the orientations of Akron's managers appropriately supported decision-making there. And, because Akron's task was so precisely defined and its behavior so rigidly controlled around the automated production lines, the high degree of coordination of effort and of colleague similarities is suitable to that unit. In contrast, Stockton's egalitarianly distributed influence and participatory type of supervision meant that decision-making tended to be sanctioned and encouraged at all levels in the formal structure. Such orientations appropriately reflected the fact that the information and knowledge needed to make critical research decisions in such an unpredictable, fast-changing environment resided in the researchers themselves and at all levels in the laboratory. And, Stockton's perceptions of differences among colleagues and of a relatively low degree of coordination of effort among colleagues reflected the fact that a wide variety of scientific disciplines and projects had to be represented in a laboratory of this kind if it were to be successful. One research manager in Stockton summed up the appropriateness of these attributes to the research task especially well:

I don't have the expert knowledge about astrophysics that one of our newest researchers has. It would be plain foolish for me to try to second-guess the kinds of projects we ought to take on in that field. So, we expect everyone in the laboratory to have a say in the things we do. . . . You can't run a place with as many different kinds of knowledge represented as we have here any other way.

It is also interesting to note that the less successful Carmel research laboratory tended to have more of the decisions made at the top of the organization, and the researchers' particular expertises did not give them much say in the laboratory's choice of projects.

Finally, the professionals in *both* Akron and Stockton perceived their chief executive to have more concern for the task than for people or relationships. This kind of managerial style seemed to us to make sense in both kinds of task environments. In Akron, the technology of the task was so pervasive and controlling that if top managerial behavior relegated concern for that technology and task to second-best, effectiveness of performance probably would have been reduced. On the other hand, knowledge concerning Stockton's task was rapidly changing and uncertain, and this called for more individualistic problem-solving behavior. However, that individualistic behavior might have become totally segmented and totally uncoordinated, causing the group to fall apart, unless the top executive tended to focus the group's attention on the overall research task via his high concern for that task.

These differences in the characteristics of climate fit in the two high performers are summarized in Table 5.2. As with the attributes of formal fit, the less-effective Hartford and Carmel sites measured a lower degree of fit with their respective tasks than did Akron and Hartford. As examples, the Hartford containers plant showed a relatively egalitarian distribution of influence, perceptions of low struc-

TABLE 5.2

Differences in the Characteristics of "Climate Fit" in Akron and Stockton

	Akron (Certain Manufacturing Task)	Stockton (Uncertain Research Task)
1. Structural orientation	Perceptions of tightly controlled behavior and high degree of structure	Perceptions of low degree of structure
2. Time orientation	Short-term	Long-term
3. Goal orientation	Manufacturing	Scientific
4. Distribution of influence	Perceptions of low total influence, concentrated at upper levels	Perceptions of high total influence, more evenly spread out among all levels
5. Character of superior-subordinate relations	Low freedom vis-à-vis superiors to choose and handle task, directive type of supervision	High freedom vis-à-vis superiors to choose and handle task, participatory type of supervision
6. Character of colleague relations	Perceptions of much similarity among colleagues, high degree of coordination of colleague effort	Perceptions of much difference among colleagues, relatively low degree of coordination of colleague effort
7. Top executive's "managerial style"	More concerned with task than people	More concerned with task than people

ture and a more participatory type of supervision. The Carmel research laboratory showed a somewhat top-heavy distribution of influence, perceptions of high structure, and a more directive type of supervision.

Sense of Competence Motivation in Akron and Stockton

Akron and Stockton were obviously quite different as places to work. In comparing and contrasting their organizational attributes, we have been stressing two interrelated points. On the one hand, although the organizational characteristics differed markedly in the two sites, such differences suited the distinctive dimensions of each task well. On the other hand, such differences in organizational characteristics led to differences in behavior in the two units, but these differences tended in both cases to result in effective task performance. Our particular concern in this study was to link the organizational characteristics that define task fit for an organization with individual motivation. What could motivate individuals in a high-fit task setting to act in a manner consistent with task unit fit, leading to effective task performance?

FIGURE 5.1

Differences in the Sense of Competence in the Containers Plant Environment

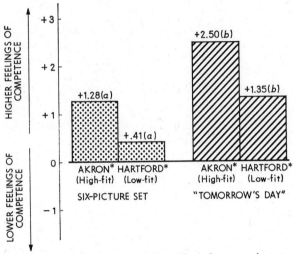

* Akron scores are the means of averages of 30 respondents. Hartford scores are the means of 32 respondents. All tests were scored and re-scored. The correlation (r) between the first score and the re-score on Part One of all the tests was .903 and on Part Two of all the tests was .882. The percent of imagery agreement between the first score and the re-score on Part One of all the tests was 91.6% and on Part Two of all the tests was 89.8%.
    (a) Statistical significance of differences in means: one-tailed probability, $t = 3.84$, $P = <.001$
    (b) Statistical significance of differences in means: one-tailed probability, $t = 3.97$, $P = <.001$

A partial answer was related to the sense of competence motivation of the professionals in both sites. Managers and professionals in Akron and Stockton showed higher feelings of competence or more of a sense of competence than did their counterparts in the lower fit Hartford and Carmel sites. In other words, the individuals in Akron and Stockton were more motivated by feelings of competence than were the individuals in Hartford and Carmel. The differences in the sense of competence for the managers and professionals in the certain manufacturing task environment (Akron and Hartford containers plants) are summarized in Figure 5.1, and these same differences in the uncertain research task environment (Stockton and Carmel communications technology laboratories) are summarized in Figure 5.2.[8] The data incorporated in these charts suggest that the individuals

---

[8] The instrument we used to measure the feelings of competence in our sites contained two parts. The first asked a participant to write creative and imaginative stories in response to six ambiguous pictures, while the second asked a participant to write a creative and imaginative story about his day on the job "tomorrow," that is, what he may be doing, thinking, and feeling "tomorrow" on his job. Instruments such as these are called "projective tests" because it is assumed that the respondent projects into his stories his own attitudes, thoughts, feelings, needs and wants, all of which can be measured from the stories.

FIGURE 5.2

Differences in the Sense of Competence in the Communications Technology
Research Environment

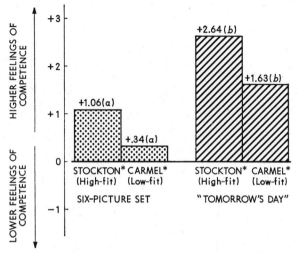

* Stockton scores are the means or averages for 25 respondents. Carmel scores are the means for 24 respondents. All tests were scored and re-scored. The correlation (4) between the first score and the re-score on Part One of all the tests was .856 and on Part Two of all the tests was .877. The percent of imagery agreement between the first score and the re-score on Part One of all the tests was 90.7% and on Part Two of all the tests was 92.4%.
(a) Statistical significance of difference in means: one-tailed probability, $t = 2.83$, $P = .01$.
(b) Statistical significance of difference in means: one-tailed probability, $t = 2.71$, $P = .01$.

in Akron and Stockton were *motivated* to perform that kind of be-havior that results from task unit fit and that leads to effective task performance precisely because such behavior was also leading to mastery of a particular task environment and, therefore, to a heightened sense of competence for them.

Summary of the Study

In its barest form, then, the major study findings seem to indicate:

1. That there is a reward in feelings of competence or a sense of competence from gaining mastery over and performing effectively in a task environment;

2. That the managers and professionals in high-fit Akron and high-fit Stockton were in task organizations whose organizational charac-teristics, although markedly different from each other, encouraged the kind of behavior that could lead, and in fact was leading, to effective and successful performance in each's particular task envi-ronment; and,

3. That the managers and professionals in Akron and Stockton were motivated to perform the kind of behavior that results from task unit fit and that leads to successful task performance because it was indeed leading to the reward in feelings of competence and mastery for them.

Our study suggests a link between organizational characteristics and individual motivation. More specifically, we found that when organizational characteristics suit the kind of task being performed, there is the likelihood of engaging and fulfilling needs for mastery and competence and the likelihood of an individual's attaining high feelings of competence or a high sense of competence. The organizational characteristics in Akron and Stockton, as were described earlier, were very different. Their common feature, though, was that in both sites such characteristics were appropriate to the differences in the task of the units. And this appropriateness was matched in both units by high sense of competence motivation of the individuals working there.

The study findings also suggest organizational characteristics to be simultaneously linked to, or interdependent with, *both* individual motivation *and* effective task performance. Akron and Stockton, the two units whose organizational characteristics suited their separate tasks well, had both been evaluated for us as highly successful performers.[9] And, we found the individuals in these high-fit, high-performing units had a high sense of competence. What our work points to, therefore, are interdependencies or links between the organizational characteristics of "fit," effective task performance, and individual sense of competence motivation. Graphically, these links can be expressed thus:

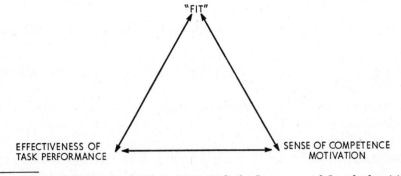

---

[9] Note that this is completely consistent with the Lawrence and Lorsch theorizing and findings in *Organization and Environment*.

Implications of the Study for Managers

This study should help managers principally by identifying major links and interdependencies to consider in designing an organization which will accomplish its task *and* provide for the needs of individuals. Our approach therefore bridges works such as Burns's and Stalker's dealing with the effective performance of structured and unstructured tasks and works such as Argyris' dealing with individual motivation. For example, we found in our two high-fit units, one with a structured, certain task and one with an unstructured, uncertain task, that such fit was associated at one and the same time with effective task performance and with high sense of competence motivation. And, although we did not focus here on the low-fit Hartford plant and the low-fit Carmel research laboratory, we can say that the lower degree of fit in both instances tended to be linked to less-effective task performance and to lower feelings of competence. As a result this study suggests organizational fit to be interdependent with both task performance and sense of competence motivation, as signified by the triangle of relationships described above.

Perhaps one of the most intriguing aspects of our findings is this probable interdependency and circularity of those three variables in the triangle: each appears to be related to the other so that manipulating one can result in a change in the others. For example, by manipulating organizational characteristics so that they suit the task better or by engaging more feelings of competence in the members of the organization, a manager may be able to improve task performance. Likewise, a manager may be able to somehow independently improve performance, which we suggest would also lead to higher feelings of competence and to individual behavior that suits the task better, as members of the organization try to maintain and add to their higher sense of competence. And, finally, a manager may be able to heighten the feelings of competence in his organization by, for example, an influx of new blood that would be challenged by the task, a move our findings indicate would probably lead to more effective performance and to a higher degree of "fit" as individuals sought to reinforce their competent behavior.

Although our primary concern has been the interdependencies among our variables, our study also seems to indicate that a manager can most easily derive the benefits of all those links by initially focusing on one of the variables, organizational "fit." We have identified certain organizational characteristics that a manager can manipulate to better suit his task. As examples, we looked at the formal practices in an organization; the time and goal orientations; the perceptions of structure, of the distribution of influence, of superior-subordinate and colleague relations, and of the top manager's "managerial style." These are all aspects of an organization that a manager can change and vary according to the requirements of the task. And, as the organizational pattern becomes more appropriate to the kind of work being done, the manager may have "locked on" to the triangle of interdependencies indentified in the study to raise the level of performance and the sense of competence motivation in his work unit.

Finally, we believe that sense of competence motivation itself has significant implications for managers because it seems to be important to individuals with very different patterns of predispositions and very different patterns of other needs and values. For example, the professionals we talked to in the Akron plant seemed to us to be quite different from those we talked to in the Stockton research laboratory. In Akron, people in general did not seem to mind the predictiveness, the certainty, the routineness of the task, or the highly structured, hierarchical organizational pattern that precluded the necessity of their making many of the critical decisions. In Stockton, on the other hand, individuals in general thrived on change and challenge, and felt comfortable only in an organization that put some of the burden of making critical decisions on them. But, the professionals in Akron, who were more comfortable with predictability and structure, and the professionals in Stockton, who were very comfortable with ambiguity and change, *all* showed significantly higher feelings of competence than their counterparts in the less-effective, lower "fit" units. A major contribution to managers, therefore, may be the study's identification and investigation of a particular need pattern concerning the sense of competence that appears to be a powerful motivator for individuals with either a high predisposition and need for structure or a high predisposition and need for autonomy.

So, in terms of the managerial dilemma of designing an organization or functional task unit to accomplish its task well and to provide for the needs of the individuals who do the work, this study points up a practical, empirically based set of links that recognizes the import of task requirements and individual needs in equal and interdependent measure.

6 | The Development of Differentiation in Organized Work*

Stanley H. Udy, Jr.

Udy has for a number of years studied organization by delving into man's past. He has carefully mined a wealth of information about organizations from the records of anthropologists on ancient and current examples of pre-industrial societies. In this article he has brought his insights and data from these sources to bear on the question of how the complex pattern of differentiation we find in modern industrial organizations has roots in early organizational forms. He finds that our patterns of differentiation are not a recent social invention. Their precursors are to be found in certain pre-industrial "contractual" organizations. His informed speculation about the reasons behind these patterns adds useful perspective to our understanding of contemporary organization forms. His findings also have implications for some of the current problems of industrialization being experienced in less well developed countries. Udy is currently professor of sociology at Yale University.

D IFFERENTIATION is perhaps one of the most obvious features of large-scale organization. Because complex organizations must deal with pluralistic environments, one type of organizational response is not sufficient and parts of organizations are separated and structured differently. These organizational subunits are intended to cope with a particular subenvironment. Most of the research con-

---

* Expanded version of a paper delivered at the annual meetings of the Academy of Management, December 1968; original version published in the *Journal of the Academy of Management*, 1969.

For a summary statement of the "classical" position, see James G. March and Herbert A. Simon, *Organizations* (New York: John Wiley & Sons, Inc., 1958), pp. 22–30.

cerned with this differentiation has concentrated on comparing and contrasting structural characteristics of organizational subunits according to the peculiar environmental problems which they face, and in doing so researchers have discovered that modern industrial firms are broadly differentiated in strikingly similar ways.[1] Brown observes, for example, that most industrial organizations are differentiated into sales, production, and research and development components, and other researchers, not to mention casual and "common sense" observers, have concurred.[2] The more general formulation of Lawrence and Lorsch analogously distinguishes the market, techno-economic, and scientific subsystems, respectively.[3] Although industrial firms have other subdivisions as well, there appears to be something truly basic about this particular tripartite division, or some generalized version of it.

Why do modern industrial firms tend to be differentiated in this particular way? We have looked at organizational differentiation in relation to social and industrial development, and found that it takes form as a result of developmental processes. An important, if at times unsung, fact of industrial development is that most work organizations in traditional society are derivative in structure from other social units, such as kinship groups and political hierarchies.[4] As a consequence, it is often rather difficult for them to be adapted to modern industrial technology. It is in the process of such adaptation that we shall seek the sources of differentiation.

Our data are based on a sample of 359 work organizations in 125 nonindustrial societies selected according to Murdock's criteria for his "World Ethnographic Sample."[5] For each society, available ethnographic materials were surveyed—using the Human Relations Area Files wherever possible—and data were abstracted on variables relevant to our analysis. Owing to gaps in the material, not all 359

---

[1] Paul R. Lawrence and Jay W. Lorsch, *Organization and Environment* (Boston: Division of Research, Graduate School of Business Administration, Harvard University, 1967).

[2] Wilfred Brown, *Explorations in Management* (London: Heinemann, 1960), pp. 143–45.

[3] Lawrence and Lorsch, *op. cit.*, pp. 28–29.

[4] Manning Nash, *Primitive and Peasant Economic Systems* (San Francisco: Chandler Publishing Co., 1966), p. 23.

[5] George P. Murdock, "World Ethnographic Sample," *American Anthropologist*, Vol. 59 (1959), pp. 664–87.

organizations, nor all 125 societies, could be used in all parts of the analysis, as is evident from the tables which follow. In each case, all organizations offering adequate data were used.[6]

THE SOCIAL DERIVATION OF TRADITIONAL WORK ORGANIZATION

In contrast to modern industrial society, where work organization is by and large expected to be adapted to physical technological requirements, most work organizations in traditional society were derived from already existing social units having functions other than work. This derivation is of three types.[7] The first is *familial*. The most simple example of this type is a family household farming its own plot of land. However, many traditional family-based work organizations are much more complex. Frequently the kinship principle is extended to include relatives other than immediate family residing in other households, with the institution of reciprocity among different families in the same community often involved as well. The Betsileo of Madagascar present a typical complex example, in their organization of wet ricefield cultivation. This operation involves raising rice plants in a nursery, and later transplanting them into a rice paddy which has been flooded with water and worked until the mud is of homogeneous consistency. The head of the family owning the field recruits the families of his male relatives, who are obliged to help as part of their kinship roles. If more workers are required, other families assist on the basis of community reciprocity expectations. The members of the work party "automatically," as it were, fall into work roles socially defined on the bases of generation and sex. The men in the youngest generation start across the field, driving cattle around in the mud to reduce the soil to an even consistency. Following immediately behind are the men of the middle generation, levelling the field with hoes. Behind them are the women of both the youngest and middle generations, planting the rice shoots. During this time, the women of the oldest generation dig up the plants from the nursery, carry them to the younger women in the field, and supervise the latter in the planting. Meanwhile, the men of the oldest generation regulate the

---

[6] This sample is the same one employed in S. H. Udy, Jr., *Work in Traditional and Modern Society* (Englewood Cliffs, N.J.: Prentice-Hall, Inc., 1969).

[7] *Ibid.*

water level and repair the dikes, while supervising the younger men in the field.[8]

The second possible foundation for socially based work is *political*. In 11th-century England, for example, agriculture was carried on in a broad context of serfdom and tenancy arrangements, with the entire process directed through landholders of superior socio-political status.[9] And in various traditional societies, differential political status could also serve as a basis for direct drafts of forced labor, under conditions varying from peonage, serfdom, and slavery, to relatively "free" political arrangements.[10] Again, the situation is similar to that of familial work, in that the work organization is not structured around a physical task, but around a pre-existent set of social considerations.

A third social basis of work organization lies in general *contractual* obligations including, but typically not restricted to, work. Sometimes agreements are concluded between proprietary parties and individuals, and sometimes between proprietary parties and other groups, such as age-grade associations. The Dahomean *dokpwe* is a classic example. It consists largely of young men cooperating in bride-work, but who also often hire themselves out, so to speak, as a supplementary work force to assist in agriculture and construction.[11] This case too shares the property of being organized on social, rather than physical-technical, grounds, though as we shall see presently the institution of contract offers the possibility of moving toward a more physical emphasis.

Two important exceptions exist to the generalization that traditional work is socially based. The first is in highly primitive societies (i.e., societies not practicing sedentary agriculture), where work organizations are by and large structured according to physical task requirements. The demand for food in non-agricultural societies is sufficiently urgent that most organized work is devoted to such activities as hunting, fishing, or collection, with these activities defined as general social goals. Work organizations are thus confronted with

---

[8] H. M. DuBois, S. J., *Monographie des Betsileo* (Paris: Institut d'Ethnologie, 1938), *passim*, but esp. pp. 434–40.

[9] Frederic Seebohm, *The English Village Community* (4th ed.; London: Longmans Green, 1905), pp. 117–25.

[10] For a more extensive discussion of such systems, see S. H. Udy, Jr., *Organization of Work* (New Haven: Human Relation Area Files Press, 1959), pp. 72–96.

[11] Melville J. Herskovits, *Dahomey* (New York: J. J. Augustin, Inc.—Publisher, 1945), pp. 63–77; 101–102.

unquestioned physical tasks to which they are expected to adapt. Furthermore, proximity to the subsistence level means that fewer complex institutional arrangements exist which could enter into work, and render it more socially based. In the absence of sedentary agriculture there is a relative lack of complex landed property arrangements. Also, hunting, fishing, and collection operations are for the most part intermittent, rather than continuous activities, so that work is simply not carried on in the same way for a sufficiently sustained period of time to result in consistent disruptions of social structure. Whaling among the traditional Aleut provides a typical example. Aleut whaling was conducted under the direction of special whaling chiefs (*toyones*) chosen by acclamation on the basis of their technical knowledge. The *toyones* would recruit and assign a work force on the basis of ability to perform technically defined tasks. Certain men, detailed as lookouts, would ascend bluffs to try to spot whale schools. After sighting a school, a lookout would give an initial signal, and boats would be launched and then deployed with coordination by further standard signals between the lookouts, the whaling chief (who by now is occupying one of the boats), and the heads of the boat crews—the man in charge of each crew having been assigned on the basis of his ability as a marksman. The strategy was to surround a whale and shoot as many harpoons into it as possible, whereupon the whale would dive, hopefully die, and within three days float to the surface. The carcass would then be sighted by lookouts, and boats would be dispatched to haul it ashore.[12]

As can be seen from the description, the organization of this operation is based on physical technological considerations. Tasks are delineated and men are recruited and assigned on the basis of technical competence. Interpersonal relations are determined by the nature of the physical work, rather than the converse.

The second exception to the prevailing social nature of traditional work lies in certain contractual work organization. A contract is, in effect, an agreement between parties to behave in a certain manner for a specified time.[13] In principle, therefore, contracts can, and sometimes do, define work relationships in purely physical terms. As a

---

[12] Henry W. Elliott, *Our Arctic Province* (New York: Charles Scribner's Sons, 1886), pp. 138–41; Waldemar Jochelson, *History, Ethnology, and Anthropology of the Aleut* (Washington, D.C.: Carnegie Institute, 1933), pp. 56–57; Ivan E. P. Veniaminov, *Zapiski ob ostrovakh Unalaskinskago otdela* (St. Petersburg: Russian-American Company, 1840), pp. 341–44.

[13] Kingsley Davis, *Human Society* (New York: The Macmillan Co., 1949), p. 470.

result, some contractual work organizations embody a mixture of physical and social bases, as, for instance, where a family proprietor hires stonemasons and carpenters to assist by practicing their respective specialties, or where mutual aid societies reassign members on technical grounds when work is performed.[14] Situations of this nature are but one step removed from full contractual recruitment and assignment on technical grounds. They are therefore very important for future industrial development, and we shall explore them in more detail presently. For the time being, however, we may observe that

TABLE 6.1
Society and Work Organization*

Societal Characteristics	Physical Base	Organizational Characteristics Social Base		
		Kinship	Political	Contractual
Primitive (no sedentary agri-culture)......................46		5	1	7
Sedentary agriculture, minimal elaboration....................28		41	14	31
Centralized political control........22		27	33	21
Stratification, exchange system at least incipient............... 0		16	35	27

* The classification of societies in Table 6.1 is a fairly standard scale-type classification designed to distinguish societies close to the subsistence level from those progressively more complex, and hence a more nearly industrial society.

not only are most work organizations socially based in traditional society, but, as work organizations progress from the subsistence level, their tendency to become socially based increases. This is shown in Table 6.1.

SOCIALLY BASED WORK AND INEFFICIENCY

We see from Table 6.1 that those traditional societies closest to industrial development are precisely those in which organized work is most strongly socially based. The problem with this situation is that socially based work organizations are more likely to be technically inefficient than those which are physically based, precisely because of the various social considerations entering into work relationships.

---

[14] René Maunier, *La Construction collective de la Maison en Kabylie* (Paris: Institut d'Ethnologie, 1926), *passim*.

This hypothesis is consistently supported by data on three measures of technical inefficiency which we were able to develop. We shall present data on only one of these measures here; namely, whether or not the work role includes activities in addition to the work itself.[15]

One would suppose, for example, that work organizations recruited on political grounds would require their members to be more concerned with the discharge of political obligations, than with work, and thus be relatively inefficient technically. Table 6.2 indicates this state of affairs in our sample. With the striking exception of contractual organization, which proves to be almost as efficient as physically based forms, socially based work organizations are indeed more inefficient.

A major problem of industrialization, therefore, would seem to be

TABLE 6.2

Efficiency of Role Content

Base of Organization	Role Content Efficient	Inefficient
Physical	47	21
Kinship	6	70
Political	4	59
Contractual	42	25

a prevailing technical inefficiency in traditional organized work. This situation has in fact been commented upon by observers of work in newly industrializing areas. The International Labour Office tells us, for example, that

In a tobacco factory in Uganda the management estimated that in the factory generally three Africans are required to produce what two Europeans can produce in Europe . . . In a textile factory in the Belgian Congo . . . , one worker operates two machines, while in Belgium one European woman operates four of the same machines . . . In Ubangi-Chari the output of Africans on various forms of masonry work was only one-third to one -fourth that of workers in France performing the same type of operation.[16]

---

[15] The other two measures involved (*a*) the number of people present relative to technological demands, and (*b*) the number of levels of authority in the organization relative to technological complexity. Data respecting these measures are presented in Udy, *Work in Traditional and Modern Society op. cit.*

[16] International Labour Office, *African Labour Survey*, Studies and Reports, New Series, No. 48 (Geneva: International Labour Office, 1958), pp. 144–46.

Social scientists who study industrial development have at times attempted to explain this state of affairs on broad cultural-psychological grounds. They have suggested that the socialization process in nonindustrial culture does not foster a predisposition toward innovation, a "need for achievement," or a "rational attitude" toward task performance.[17] We are frankly inclined to be suspicious of such explanations, if only because they do not account for the relatively high degree of work efficiency found in very primitive societies. But one need not discount such explanations entirely to observe that if work is culturally defined as being socially based it will not be carried on with a high degree of technical efficiency, quite irrespective of any broader attitudinal predispositions of the workers. At least part of the solution, therefore, to the problem of inefficiency in organized work in developing societies, would seem to lie in somehow bringing about a re-definition of the work situation so that the work organization would be more directly oriented to solving physical problems rather than social ones.

Such a course is rendered all the more necessary by the central importance of technology per se in modern industrial production. Modern industrial firms are expected to base their actual operations on technological considerations. In this respect they are rather like highly primitive work organizations. But there is a very important difference. In the case of primitive work, objectives are culturally given, and the particular technology followed is specific to those given objectives. A Plains Indians buffalo hunting party is not expected, for example, to decide whether or not to hunt buffalo; the people involved already know that this is what they are supposed to be doing. But such is not the case with modern industrial work. There, the initial technological orientation is very general, as it includes an entire institutional system of science and technology. The firm is expected to make its own decisions about production objectives from a broad range of technologically possible alternatives. But such decisions cannot be made on the basis of technology alone. Decisions as to which particular objectives to pursue must ultimately be made on the basis of social values, the most common ones in modern industry having to do with profitability or similar economic criteria, though a variety of political and broader social considerations may enter into the picture

---

[17] See, for example, David C. McClelland, *The Achieving Society* (Princeton, N.J.: D. Van Nostrand Co., Inc., 1961); Everett E. Hagen, *On the Theory of Social Change* (Homewood, Ill.: The Dorsey Press, 1962).

as well. The point is that modern industry is constrained by physical considerations in a direct way, and by certain social considerations at the same time. Industrialization thus involves a return to a physically based work organization, and also entails a retention of some of the social bases of production prevailing in traditional society.

The central difficulty with this situation is that physical and social considerations in work are always at some point at odds with each other. If any work organization is to be oriented to both sets of considerations at once, it must therefore differentiate the physical environment of work from its social environment, and deal with both environments separately by specializing the parts of the work organization. Herein lies a major source of differentiation in modern industrial work.

CONTRACTURAL WORK AND DIFFERENTIATION

Contractual forms of work organization are highly critical, if not indeed crucial, in bringing about this basic differentiation in organized work. It proved possible to classify most of the socially based work organizations in our sample according to whether: (1) members were simply present on diffuse grounds; (2) members were consistently assigned to specific jobs; or (3) the specific jobs were grouped so that people involved in complexes of technological roles were concretely separated from people involved in complexes of purely social roles (for example, the people expected to deal with the "public," external to the organization, are different from the people who are actually doing the work). We found that kinship based and politically based work organizations were mostly of the diffuse type, with an occasional instance—likely to be politically based—of the job-specific variety, and essentially no instances of clear separation of technological and social roles. Contractual organizations, however, presented an entirely different picture. Contracts, in principle, are very flexible, and, unlike kinship or political obligations, can define highly specific complexes of jobs. The comparative data on efficiency already presented in Table 6.2 suggests that contractual organizations do succeed in specializing physical functions from social functions. Table 6.3 shows that such is indeed the case, and suggests further that such differentiation accounts for their relative efficiency.

Thus far we have dealt only with a general differentiation between technological and social roles in the work situation. What effect, now, does this development of a generalized physical vs. social differentiation have upon the further specialization of subunits concerned with goal setting, and with working out general technological possibilities.

TABLE 6.3

Type of Contractual Organization and
Efficiency of Role Content

Type of Contractual Organization	Role Content	
	Efficient	Inefficient
Diffuse...............	9	15
Job-specific.............	10	1
Technological vs. social.............	6	0

Table 6.4 shows that contractual organization in itself is apt to involve specialized goal setting. In addition, as differentiation of technological from social concerns takes place, contractual forms are likely to entail a further specialization of general technological concerns from specific production matters.

Kinship based and politically based work organizations do not exhibit the above specialization, except to a very limited degree; some politically based units do specialized goal setting, particularly if they are also job-specific. But no kinship or political forms showed any further differentiation. Only contractual forms appear to have a tendency to become truly differentiated internally, developing specialized

TABLE 6.4

Type of Contractual Organization and
Specialization of Subunits

Type of Contractual Organization	Specialization of Subunits		
	None	Goal Setting vs. Other	Goal Setting vs. General Tech. vs. Specific Tech. vs. Other
Diffuse...............	9	19	0
Job-specific.............	0	13	2
Technological vs. social.............	0	1	7

orientations to particular external subenvironments. Our data have shown that such forms have a tendency to become internally differentiated into four subunits: (1) a subunit relating production objectives to the social setting; (2) a subunit concerned with exploring general technological possibilities; (3) a subunit engaged in actual production; and (4) a residual subunit, involved in integrating the system in light of values deriving from an amalgam of further social concerns. This result would appear to be a general case of the pattern of minimal differentiation found to be typical of modern industry, namely, (1) marketing and sales; (2) research and development; (3) production; and (4) executive integrative components.

EXTERNAL CAUSES

It is clear that not all work organizations are differentiated in the way described above, even under conditions which we have argued to be conducive to such differentiation. It remains therefore to discover those external forces which promote such differentiation. Table 6.5 suggests that general social development may influence *contractual* work organizations in this direction. The historical cases at our dis-

TABLE 6.5

Society and Contractual Work

| Social Characteristics | Type of Contractual Organization | | |
	Diffuse	Job-Specific	Technological vs. Social
Primitive, or sedentary agriculture with minimal elaboration	14	6	1
Centralized political control	6	5	1
Stratification, exchange system at least incipient	9	4	6

posal suggest, too, that the development of commercialization and general media of exchange is critical in this process. Money is, in principle, infinitely subdivisible, and can thus aid in institutionalizing any imposed physical differentiation pattern which might lack a firm traditional social base.

General social development does not, however, have the same effect on non-contractual forms of work organization; beyond the rather limited points which we have indicated, such forms simply do not tend to be differentiated, in any social setting. Table 6.1 shows that kinship based work organization tends to decline with social development. But the same table also indicates that the relative frequency of politically based work organization increases with social development, along with contractual forms. And politically based work organizations are not subject to the tendencies toward differentiation which we have demonstrated for contractual forms. By and large, they remain diffuse in structure, undifferentiated, and hence neither especially oriented to technology nor very efficient (see Table 6.2). What determines whether a society will take the "political road" or the "contractual road" in organized work?

As yet our answer must be incomplete. Frequently both forms exist alongside one another, possibly serving different general social functions, though this is not clear. The few historical development examples at our disposal suggest one clue, however. It appears that contractual organization is rarely the initial or preferred form. It is, rather, something "resorted to" in the face of a breakdown of the effective supply of political forced labor. Slavery is cheaper than hired help, or at least people making decisions about labor recruitment in traditional society think it is. If contractual forms are to get a start initially, there must be a shortage of forced labor, and/or the political system must be too weak to recruit it. At the same time, though, the political system must be strong enough to enforce contractual obligations and to provide sufficient stability to sustain them through time.

Thus the development of work forms suited to industrialism would seem to rest on rather precarious prerequisites. It is not uncommon, for example, for contractual forms to develop complete with working for pay, only to have the entire system later revert to a political basis through debt peonage.[18] But if contractual work organization can be sustained it tends to become differentiated in the same way as modern industrial firms. It would also appear that this pattern of differentiation rests on more fundamental bases than ordinary administrative planning or a simple division of labor into complementary specialities, since it results from adaptation to conflicting environmental pressures inherent in the performance of an activity which is both physical and social at the same time. And because of the intrinsic conflicts involved, the administrative integration of the modern industrial firm would seem to be much more than a simple, routine problem.

---

[18] See, for example, Max Cary, A History of Rome (London: Macmillan, 1935), pp. 259–60, 451–52, 561–62, 666 ff.; William E. Heitland, Agricola (Cambridge: University Press, 1921), pp. 151 ff.; H. F. Pelham, Essays on Roman History (Oxford: Clarendon Press, 1911), pp. 300 ff.; Ann K. Lambton, Landlord and Peasant in Persia (London: Oxford University Press, 1953), pp. 4–7, 120; Richard L. Bowen, Jr., "The Dhow Sailor," The American Neptune (Salem, Mass.), Vol. 9 (1951), pp. 161–202.

7 | Environmental and Technological Determinants of Organizational Design

Jay Galbraith

In this paper Galbraith examines the relationships between various integrative mechanisms and the requirements for interdependence in a large aerospace firm. Drawing on data collected at the Boeing Company, he analyzes the structure and coordination processes as a function of the technology of designing and manufacturing commercial aircraft, prior to 1964. Then he describes a change in the environment which occurred in 1964 and traces the way the organization adjusted to integrative mechanisms and practices to deal with the new situation. In addition to the light this study throws on the comparative selection of integrative devices, it also suggests that the contingency approach to the study of organization can be useful in understanding the dynamics of organizational change. Galbraith is an assistant professor at the Alfred P. Sloan School of Management, Massachusetts Institute of Technology.

THE relationship between an organization's technology and its structure has become a major focus of empirical[1] and theoretical[2] work in organization theory. Lawrence and Lorsch used cross-sectional data to show that for a given environment, firms vary in their effectiveness by the degree to which they adopt coordinating mechanisms appropriate to their environments. It was also shown that these coordination devices appear with the decreasing stability of different environments.

[1] Paul R. Lawrence and Jay W. Lorsch, *Organization and Environment* (Boston: Division of Research Harvard Business School, 1967).

[2] James D. Thompson, *Organizations in Action* (New York: McGraw-Hill Book Co., 1967).

This study examines changes in organization structure which take place in response to changes in a particular environment. The first section of this chapter analyzes the structure and coordination processes as a function of technology, illustrating the concepts developed by James D. Thompson. These concepts, which concern interdependence, structure, and coordination, are described in greater detail below. The environmental change is then explained, and the changes in organization structure and process are related to this environmental change.

The organization studied was the Commercial Airplane Division of the Boeing Company in Seattle, Washington. The Commercial Airplane Division organization is represented in Figure 7.1.

FIGURE 7.1

Commercial Airplane Division Organization Chart

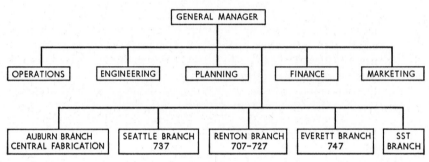

Most of the positions represented are manned by personnel of a vice-presidential status. The first line shows the division functional staff and the second line represents the operating branches. The Auburn branch acts in a support capacity, fabricating parts which cannot be economically produced by the product branches. The other branches (product branches) are responsible for the design, fabrication, and assembly of an aircraft type and are the focus of this study.

STRUCTURE AND COORDINATION OF THE PRODUCT BRANCHES BEFORE CHANGE

The product branches have the responsibility for designing and building the aircraft assigned to them, by converting aerodynamic equations and wind-tunnel data into airplanes. Figure 7.2 diagrams the sequence of steps in the process.

The product branch receives the preliminary design from product development after the decision is made to introduce the model. The first step is to do the detailed design of the aircraft down to each part and subassembly. The next step depends on whether a part is to be produced internally or externally. If produced externally, the purchasing department takes over upon completion of the design effort to begin acquisition of the part. (Some items such as engines are designed as well as produced externally.) If it is to be produced inter-

FIGURE 7.2

Work Flow at a Product Branch

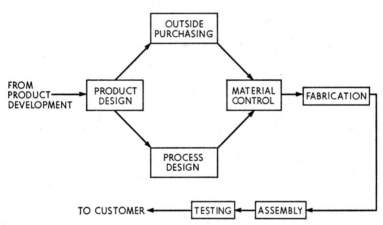

nally, the process design engineers must create the necessary manufacturing plans and tooling designs for the fabrication and subsequent assembly operations.

Following the design and acquisition steps, the material control function distributes the material and manufacturing plans for the sequential production operations. They monitor progress of parts and subassemblies and perform the necessary paperwork for reordering. Since each plane consists of about 100,000 parts, this is no simple task.

After the material has been acquired and the manufacturing methods are designed, the actual fabrication begins. Several fabricated parts are collected and joined as a subassembly. Next is a quality control inspection. This same sequence then repeats until subassemblies become major subsections which are joined in the final assembly area. The plane is then rolled out onto the field where final installations are made and preflight inspection takes place. The completed aircraft is flight tested, certified by the FAA, accepted and flown away by the customer.

This process is repeated for each customer. Although each customer may purchase a 707 with the same external structure, the interiors and electronics systems need to be modified. The different locations of food serving units necessitate the restressing of floors. In addition, each airline has pilots trained on different navigation equipment. Some foreign airlines have interior equipment in metric measurements. This means that there is substantial redesign of the product and therefore redesign of the process for each customer. When a new aircraft model is introduced, the sequence shown in Figure 7.2 is a major undertaking.

The process described above takes from a little over a year to about two years, depending, among other things, on the amount of custom designing. For the introduction of a new aircraft, the sequence to design, produce, and test requires about three years. The cost to the customer ranges from several million for a 737 to around 20 million for a 747. A typical production rate would be about ten aircraft a month in the mature stages of development.

Interdependence, Coordination, and Structure

In the development of concepts concerning interdependence, structure, and coordination, James Thompson[3] has hypothesized that the type of organization structure and form of coordination depend upon the type of interdependence contained in the task. Thompson has identified three types of interdependence, which are illustrated schematically in Figure 7.3.

The first and most simple type is *pooled* interdependence (*a*). Departments having pooled interdependence affect each other only to the extent that they share the same pool of resources or affect a common constraint in an additive manner. For example, all product design engineers designing parts and subassemblies are interdependent due to a constraint on total weight of the airplane. Weight must

---

[3] *Ibid.*, chap. 5.

be below a specified amount in order to meet the customer specifications for speed, range, and operating economy. The interdependence is pooled because weight used by one designer is not available for use by another designer. But neither designer affects the other except through this constraint, which is *additive*.

Two departments have *sequential* interdependence (*b*) when the output of one department is the input to the other. A good example is the fabricating shop feeding an assembly shop. The parts must be cut and machined before they are assembled into more complex components. These sequences are technologically determined. The departments that have sequential interdependence also have pooled interdependence.

FIGURE 7.3

Types of Interdependencies

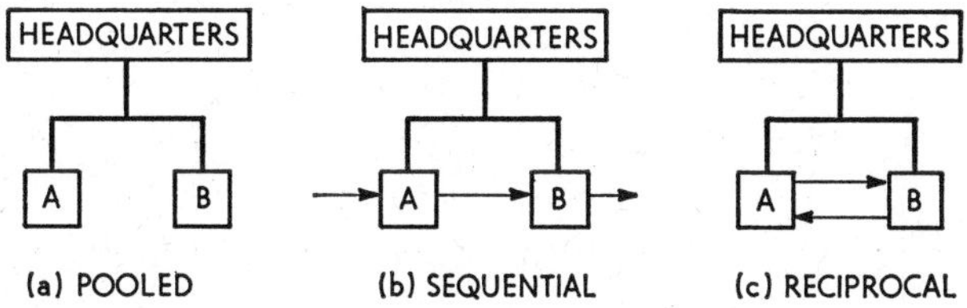

(a) POOLED   (b) SEQUENTIAL   (c) RECIPROCAL

The third type is *reciprocal* interdependence (*c*). Two units whose operations directly affect the other are reciprocally interdependent. A process and a product designer are reciprocally interdependent. Clearly, a process to produce a part cannot be designed until the part is designed. The process depends very much on the shape and material of the part. However, if the product is to be produced economically, the product should be modified to facilitate cheaper methods of production. Inputs from both designers are needed to affect the final design. It should be noted that reciprocal interdependence also implies sequential and pooled interdependence as well.

Thompson's second set of concepts concerns the types of coordination and their matching with the types of interdependence. The first type of coordination can be achieved by *standardization*.

This involves the establishment of routines or rules which constrain action of each unit or position into paths consistent with those taken by others in the interdependent relationship. An important assumption in coordination by standardization is that the set of rules be internally consistent, and this requires that the situations to which they apply be relatively stable, repetitive and few enough to permit matching of situations with appropriate rules.[4]

A second type is coordination by *plan*. The planning process involves the establishment of schedules and targets to govern the actions of the interdependent units. Planning is appropriate to more dynamic situations than is standardization. Plans quite often consist of changing the parameters in established decision rules.

The third type of coordination is *mutual adjustment*. This ". . . involves the transmission of new information during the process of action." The task is sufficiently unpredictable that pre-established decision rules and plans cannot be prepared. Thus as the predictability of the task changes the appropriate form of coordination changes from standardization to planning to mutual adjustment. Also the burden on the decision and information systems increases as the form changes from standardization to mutual adjustment. In terms of organizational resources expended, mutual adjustment is the most costly and standardization is the least costly.

One of Thompson's main propositions is that there is a distinct parallel between the types of coordination and the types of interdependence. This means that standardization is used in the most simple form—that of pooled interdependence. Schedules and plans are appropriate for sequential interdependence, while mutual adjustment is the appropriate form for reciprocal interdependence.

The organization design problem can be stated as two hypotheses. *The first is that organizations structure themselves so as to minimize coordination costs.* It follows that the first priority is given to reciprocally interdependent activities which require mutual adjustment coordination mechanisms. These positions are grouped together first to facilitate the ongoing communication processes. Next, attention is given to sequentially interdependent units. These are grouped together. Last, units with pooled interdependence are grouped together if any units remain.

The second hypothesis is that organizations group together activities of like kinds of work in order to achieve the benefits of process specialization.[5] By grouping together all work requiring machinists, the organization can produce all work requiring machining with the

---

[4] *Ibid.*, p. 56.

[5] James G. March and Herbert A. Simon, *Organization* (New York: John Wiley & Sons, Inc., 1958), p. 25.

fewest number of machinists. Process specialization increases the utilization of the means of production. Also, by grouping together like activities the volume of work performed in a given place is increased. According to Adam Smith, "the division of labor is limited by the extent of the market."[6] Thus process specialization allows a finer division of labor and therefore the use of specialized means of production and greater technical expertise.

These two propositions define the organization design problem because usually these two bases for departmentalizing an organization structure will conflict. The design problem is one of balancing the benefits of process specialization against the costs of coordination. Process specialization is important for effective performance on subtasks while coordination is important for integrating all the subtasks for effective completion of the whole task. Lawrence and Lorsch have recently stated this problem in a little different form as seeking integration without sacrificing differentiation.[7]

Structure and Coordination at a Product Branch

The organization structure at a product branch can be viewed as an illustration of the design propositions given above. First, we can

TABLE 7.1
Reciprocally Interdependent Dyads

Actors	Source
1. Product designer–product designer	Integrity of design and compatibility of parts
2. Product design–process design	Producibility of parts designs
3. Product design–purchasing	Availability of new devices and technology
4. Product design–factory	Discovery of design flaws and quality rejects
5. Process design–factory	Discovery of process design flaws and improvements

examine those activities at a product branch which have reciprocal interdependence and require the more costly forms of coordination. Table 7.1 lists some of the most important types of reciprocally interdependent dyads and the source of their interdependence.

---

[6] Adam Smith, *The Wealth of Nations* (New York: Modern Library, 1937).

[7] Lawrence and Lorsch, *op. cit.*, chap. 2.

There are five sources of reciprocal interdependence. Clearly, this is too large a grouping for mutual adjustment to coordinate the activities, but Thompson's comments about hierarchy suggest a solution.

On occasion, reciprocal interdependence is so extensive that to link all of the involved positions into one group would overtax communication mechanisms. When this occurs, organizations rank-order the interdependent positions in terms of the amount of contingency each poses for the others. Those with the greatest intercontingency form a group, and the resulting groups are then clustered into an overarching second-order group.[8]

Thus the interdependent pairs in Table 7.1 were rank-ordered by criticalness, the first pair, product designer–product designer, being most critical. Meeting the customer design specifications and the FAA safety standards are clearly the top priority goals, and so the product designers are grouped together. But even here there are too many people to form one group. Thus there is a wing department which is subdivided into various sections. The smallest group consists of those engineers that design parts that must fit together to form an assembly. The holes for rivets and fasteners must line up with fairly close tolerances. Likewise the wing must fit onto the body. However, once the points of attachment have been determined, the wing and body designers can function independently of one another. However, as design problems arise the attachment points may need to be changed, necessitating some mutual adjustment. But the amount of contingency between body and wing is not as great as between successive wing sections. Figure 7.4 shows the engineering department which is grouped to exhaust the reciprocal interdependence of type 1 in Table 7.1. Each level of hierarchy contains reciprocal interdependence but the contingency between units on a level decreases at each higher level. Although all engineers are organized into one unit, some process specialization is sacrificed to achieve integrity of design to meet all necessary specifications. Also as organization size increases, the marginal gains from process specialization get smaller and coordination costs get larger.[9] The design effort on a new aircraft consists of about 2,000 men.

Among the remaining sources of reciprocal interdependence, there is no clear priority. However, different methods of handling these independencies can be identified. The first method applies to the

---

[8] Thompson, *op. cit.*, p. 59.
[9] March and Simon, *op. cit.*, p. 29.

FIGURE 7.4

Design Engineering Organization

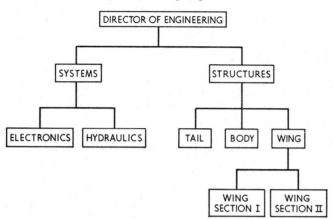

interdependence between product design and process design. Recall from the previous section that product designs are an input to the process design and process design considerations are an input to the product design. In order to achieve a product that meets customer specifications and can be produced at a reasonable cost, some mutual adjustment must take place. It seems logical that this interdependence would be handled by a continued elaboration of the hierarchy to form an all encompassing engineering group as indicated in Figure 7.5. However, this is not the case, and it will be shown later that process design is part of the manufacturing organization.

The strategy for handling the product design-process design interdependence has been to eliminate it before a project is assigned to a

FIGURE 7.5

Engineering Structure to Handle Reciprocal Interdependence between Product and Process Design

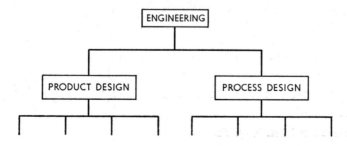

product branch. In Figure 7.2 the work flow indicates that product development is the first step. It is in this division group that the reciprocal interdependence between product design, process design, and marketing is worked out. It is identical to processes described by Lawrence and Lorsch in the plastic firms.[10] Mutual adjustment is facilitated by fewer people and fewer time constraints.

However, some additional provision for mutual adjustment must be made, since planned design always runs into unforeseen problems requiring changes. To handle such mutual adjustment around unfore-

FIGURE 7.6

Process Design Organization

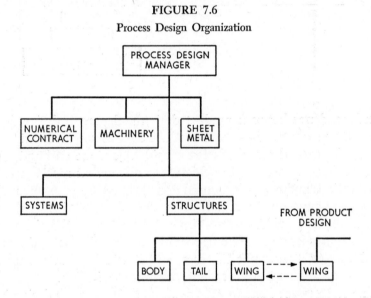

seen changes, some process specialization is sacrificed. If process design did not have to coordinate with other functions, it would be organized around process specialties such as numerical control, plastic molding, sheet metal work, parts machining, etc. Instead, as shown in Figure 7.6, the process design organization reflects the product design organization. This facilitates direct contact between designers and first line managers. These are the people who are conversant with the problems and can make the necessary adjustments. The process specialties are represented as staff advisors. This represents a compromise between the costs of coordination and benefits of process special-

---

[10] Lawrence and Lorsch, *op. cit.*

ization. This structure also facilitates the handling of sequential interdependence.

This arrangement permits mutual adjustment when only a limited amount is needed because of preplanning between process and product development and marketing. This was the case for the 707 and the 727 airplanes. The 707 had a prototype designed, built, and tested before undertaking the final design and production. The 727 had four years of development and wind-tunnel testing before final design. A good deal of the reciprocal interdependence was worked out in this manner. In addition, the product design group was experienced from previous airplane designs and learned how to modify designs for economic manufacture. For these reasons, interaction was not often needed even though interdependence was present.

The reciprocal interdependence between product design and purchasing was handled in a little different manner. Some mutual adjustment took place in product development where purchasing is also represented. Additional mutual adjustment is necessary as problems arise and as new technology becomes available in the market. Like process design, purchasing does not form a second order grouping with product design. Unlike process design, however, purchasing's organization is not a mirror image of product design. Instead, the purchasing organization is divided into units which deal with homogeneous groupings of vendors.[11] This is more important for the performance of the purchasing function. The mutual adjustment takes place in two ways. There is some direct contact between product designers and purchasing, but the structure does not encourage establishment of close relationships. The other method is with a group that maintains contact with the market and the engineers and suggests changes.

Liaison Departments as Integrating Mechanisms

The last type of reciprocal interdependence exists between the process and product design groups and the factory. In converting a paper airplane to a metal airplane some of the design assumptions prove faulty. The foreman discovers parts that do not fit in the tools or that fail to fit each other. This may be due to faulty workmanship, faulty product design, faulty process design, or some combination.

---

[11] Thompson, *op. cit.*, p. 70.

When these problems arise, there is need for mutual adjustment to redesign process or product. Both design groups handle this interdependence in the same way: They establish liaison departments in their organizations and station the liaison engineers in the factory.

FIGURE 7.7

Product Design Organization

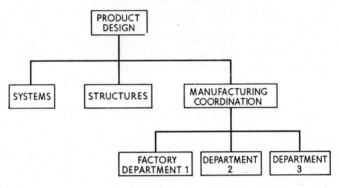

FIGURE 7.8

Variation of Integrating Personnel with Task Certainty

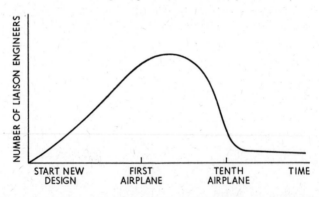

Figure 7.7 illustrates the structure of these groups, which are organized to assist factory departments rather than by engineering specialty. If difficult design problems arise, they are taken back to the design groups.

These liaison departments serve an integrating function.[12] Research has shown that the number of such integrators varies directly with the certainty of the task, and Figure 7.8 shows how the number builds

---

[12] Lawrence and Lorsch, *op. cit.*

after the start of the design of a new aircraft.[13] It peaks when all the parts arrive and assembly begins. The number drops off to a sustaining force after about the first ten aircraft are complete. In this case, too, mutual adjustment takes place through a structural arrangement.

Sequential Interdependence

This exhausts the major sources of reciprocal interdependence. Each of the sources have structural arrangements to facilitate the mutual adjustment of the interdependent groups. Following Thompson's propositions, the next step is to look at sequential interdependence, the next most costly to coordinate.

After grouping units to minimize coordination by mutual adjustment, organizations under norms of rationality seek to place sequentially interdependent groups tangent to one another, in a cluster which is localized and conditionally autonomous.[14]

It is at this point that an interesting design choice arises. Since planning is the form of coordination used for sequential interdependence and planning costs increase with growth in the number of variables and length of lines of communication, it is expected that organizations will place the planning job in the smallest possible cluster of serially interdependent units. If this was the case a product branch organization would appear like Figure 7.9.

The wing organization has the serial interdependence depicted in Figure 7.2 and there is little interaction with other components (body, tail, etc.) until final assembly. Thus these components could do their own scheduling with the product design departments.

The price of such an organization is the loss of process specialization benefits. This is particularly true in purchasing and fabrication. In purchasing there will be common vendors in each group and therefore duplicate contacts. In fabrication there is expensive equipment which must be fully utilized, and duplication is costly. As a result, the organization is structured as shown in Figure 7.10.

---

[13] This is consistent with recent additional findings by Lawrence and Lorsch where the percentage of special integrating personnel varied with the certainty of the task and the type of interdependence. In their study the plastic firms had 22%, the food processers 17%, and the container firms 0%. See Jay W. Lorsch and Paul R. Lawrence, "Environmental Factors and Organization Integration," paper prepared for the Annual Meeting of the American Sociological Association, August 27, 1968, Boston, Mass.

[14] Thompson, *op. cit.*, p. 58.

FIGURE 7.9

Product Branch with Sequentially Interdependent Clusters

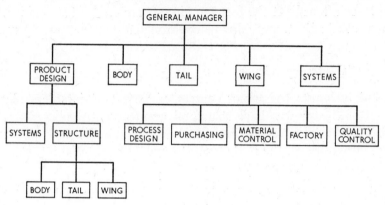

Manufacturing represents a first-order grouping of sequentially interdependent units. The product branch under the general manager becomes a second-order grouping of sequentially interdependent units.

The organization of Figure 7.10 gains complete utilization of production facilities but at the cost of increasing the difficulty of coordinating the work flow. With planning and scheduling as the means of coordination for sequential interdependence, the coordination costs increase as the number of variables and the amount of communication increase. Some process specialization is sacrificed within a function to reduce these coordination costs. It was mentioned earlier that process design was organized to facilitate interaction with product design to resolve both reciprocal and sequential interdependence.

FIGURE 7.10

Functional Organization of Product Branch—Before Change

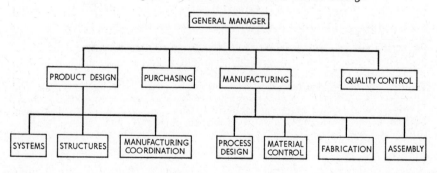

Also, purchasing was departmentalized so as to facilitate interaction with homogeneous vendor groupings. If in addition the material control, fabrication, assembly, and quality control were each departmentalized so as to best perform their subtasks, the number of separate departments through which an order must pass would get very large. The scheduling and sequencing problems would be complex. Thus the material control and quality control functions are departmentalized internally on the same basis as the fabricating and assembly departments. This gives some continuity to the work flow, reduces the number of variables in the scheduling problem, and facilitates direct managerial contact for adjacent functional supervisors.

The scheduling job is still quite substantial. After product design, orders must pass through purchasing, process design, fabrication, and assembly, which are organized on different bases. Process design and assembly are quite similar, however. The communication costs would be substantial if frequent reporting of all orders in all departments were required. However, the communication costs have been reduced by adding slack time between the start and finish of the design, produce, and test sequence. The effect is to add delays in the flow between functions. This takes the form of order backlogs for paper processing functions and in-process inventories for parts processing functions. This uncoupling of sequential functions greatly reduces the frequency of reporting and the need for rescheduling. Problems arising in one function are less likely to affect the operations of other functions. When they do, the organization hierarchy, direct contact of affected supervisors, and rescheduling can handle it. Thus the inventory and backlog buffers reduce the amount of information processing and decision-making needed for effective integration.

The scheduling task itself is performed by departments within product design and manufacturing. The group within manufacturing schedules the work flow from process design to quality control. The group within product design handles the sequential interdependence between the design groups. In addition, these two groups along with one in purchasing are partially responsible for the sequential interdependence between the functions in the product branch.

The Program Manager's Office

There is one additional department which enters into the scheduling process. (See Figure 7.11.) This is the program manager's office. This group collects information for the general manager and aids in

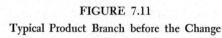

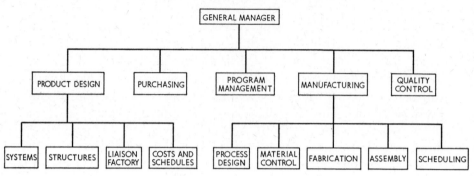

FIGURE 7.11

Typical Product Branch before the Change

the integration of the functions. In addition, the program manager maintains information needed by marketing and represents the branch to the customer. The program manager chairs a committee consisting of the functional scheduling groups and marketing. This committee decides on internal start and finish dates for each customer order. These dates become the schedule that handles the second-order sequential interdependence. Then each group breaks out more detailed schedules for start and finish dates within each function.

This method of coordination works very well as long as every department meets its due date. The addition of slack time mentioned before allows for this. It is only when due dates are missed that additional coordination effort is needed. There are two possible types of schedule disruption which require additional coordination effort —predictable and unpredictable.

The predictable disruptions result from the constant flow of design changes coming from product design engineers. The design changes are caused by attempts to update technology, by rejects from quality control, by liaison engineers, and by customer requests. Since design changes originate in the product design step, a change can affect all subsequent functional activity. The additional coordination effort takes the form of a committee called a change board. Each function including sales has a permanent representative on the board. They meet daily to discuss schedule and budget changes. The changes are then communicated to the affected groups.

The unpredictable schedule disruptions usually arise from uncertainties in task performance. The uncertainty varies between functions. The design groups have the greatest uncertainty, and the uncertainty varies with the maturity of the project and the state of the art of the design. Thus the introduction of new models introduces the greatest uncertainty. What makes the problem difficult is that the schedule disruptions are most likely to occur in the design functions which are at the start of the sequential work flow. Therefore they can potentially disrupt all subsequent activity. Some of the disruptions can be handled by direct managerial contact, by rescheduling, and through the hierarchy. But when numerous problems arise, the deci-

FIGURE 7.12

Stockout History of Commercial Airplane Division

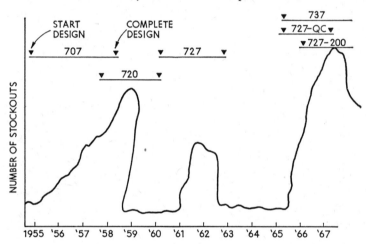

sion-making capacity of the organization is exceeded. One measure of the goodness of the sequential coordination is the number of stockouts. A stockout occurs if a part or assembly is not available for installation as scheduled. Stockouts significantly increase labor costs. Figure 7.12 gives the stockout history of the Commercial Airplane Division.

This figure illustrates quite graphically the effect of uncertainty on organizational performance. Periods of high stockouts coincide perfectly with the introduction of new models. Thus the sequential coordination strategy and structure just described are best suited for stable tasks. The high levels of stockouts were tolerated temporarily and the organization returned to normal performance after the completion of the first few aircraft. This was judged as less costly than adding additional coordination effort or changing structure (as suggested in Figure 7.9) to self-contain some of the sequential interdependence. This performance problem was the price paid for process specialization in the purchasing and manufacturing functions.

Thus the primary problem of a product branch is the scheduling of sequentially interdependent activities when the initial activities are highly unprogrammed. This scheduling is accomplished by scheduling departments, scheduling committees, and the use of order backlogs and in-process inventories. Some process specialization is sacrificed in non-critical activities to reduce the size of the scheduling problem. Also the backlogs and inventories reduce the communication costs.

There is also a good deal of coordination by standardization. Routines exist for monitoring the flow of the 100,000 parts through the sequence of functions. Another routine is called configuration management. This guarantees that the aircraft actually assembled is identical to the specifications given by the customer. Otherwise the wrong equipment could be placed in it as the aircraft goes through all the functions over a two-year period.

ENVIRONMENTAL CHANGES

A product branch as described above is a complex organization. It makes use of all the coordination devices referred to by Lawrence and Lorsch: integrating liaison departments, scheduling departments, scheduling committees, direct managerial contact, superior-subordinate contact, and an extensive paper work system.

During the period 1963, 1964, and 1965 some significant changes took place at Boeing. First, the Commercial Airplane Division completed its transition from military to commercial business. Second, the enormous increase in commercial air traffic increased the demand for commercial aircraft. This necessitated a rapid build-up of men, material, and facilities, without the financial assistance provided by gofernment contracts. (The government always made progress payments to finance build-ups of this nature, but until recently the commercial airlines did not.)

The third and most significant change took place in the market. With the 707 Boeing had to demonstrate the efficiency of jet aircraft over propeller aircraft in the commercial market. Success brought direct competition from Douglas' DC-8 and Convair's 880.

When Boeing introduced the 727 the problem was to establish a market for jet aircraft in the medium range routes. Douglas' response this time was not direct competition but a new short-range aircraft, the DC-9.

After 1964 the problem facing Boeing was not to establish a market but to meet opportunities as quickly as possible. The introduction of the short-range 737, the new versions of the 727, the giant jet 747, and the SST, all took place under competitive pressures from the DC-9, an elongated DC-9, a commercial derivative of Lockheed's C-5A, the stretched version of the DC-8, and the British-French Concorde.

This new situation meant that longer lead time was no longer an effective method of absorbing uncertainty and reducing scheduling costs. The financial constraints were against accumulating in-process inventories and the market constraints favored reducing lead time rather than increasing it. Also, the 737 and 747 received less time in product development than the 707 and 727, leaving more problem-solving and hence greater uncertainty for the design-production sequence. Boeing's response to these environmental changes is described below.

RESPONSES TO ENVIRONMENTAL CHANGE

In the 1966–67 period interfunctional changes took place at the product branches in designing and manufacturing the aircraft. The environmental changes had a direct impact on the strategy for coordinating functions. Reaching the market quickly meant less research and development effort. Since increased lead time was no longer an acceptable method of uncoupling the sequential functions, the uncertainty of the task was increased and simultaneously the system became more vulnerable to uncertainty-caused schedule disruptions. The branches were faced with design choices which consisted of strategies that allowed acceptance of increased numbers of stockouts, that increased coordination effort, or that consisted of changes in structure which reduced the need for coordination. The response was primarily increased coordination effort. Major structure changes were avoided because the periods of high uncertainty were temporary.

The 1966–67 period was one of unusually high stockout activity, as was shown in Figure 7.12. It was also during this period that stockouts slowed production and subsequently caused a financial crisis at Boeing's principle competitor, the Douglas Company. This fact helped eliminate possible strategies to accept higher levels of stock-outs.

The Liaison Group

The first coordination mechanism was added between product design and process design. It was here that the uncertainties were the greatest and there was both reciprocal and sequential interdependence. The additional coordination was performed by a liaison group of process designers who were physically stationed in the product design area. Their first responsibility was to work with the product designer and suggest design alternatives which would allow less costly manufacturing processes. Due to the environmental changes, the reciprocal interdependence required communication and interaction to achieve the necessary coordination. This was due to several factors. First, the reciprocal interdependence was not completely worked out in product development. Second, the amount of communication exceeded the capacity of direct managerial contact. And finally the increased volume of activity brought in new engineers who were not familiar with past practices. These combined to create a need for liaison engineers.

The liaison group also aided in the coordination of sequential interdependence. If the product designers were late in completing a design, this delayed the start of the process design activity. In order to put a part back on schedule, the process design group would have to resort to overtime. However, the liaison men took advantage of the fact that a part design did not have to be 100% complete before the process design could begin. The tool design could be started if rough dimensions and material were known. Thus the liason engineers kept the process designers supplied with work by bringing them partially completed parts design. In this way the design efforts were run in parallel rather than in series with the liaison man as the communication link.

Thus the liaison group facilitated mutual adjustment and allowed the removal of slack time from the schedule without causing disruptions. The liaison group also represented an increase in coordination costs since it was used in addition to, not instead of, the schedule and direct managerial contact. However, once the design of the new aircraft was complete, the liaison men resumed normal duties as process designers or liaison men elsewhere. The activity was needed only in periods of high uncertainty.

The Task Force

The second type of coordination device used was the task force. The task force groups provided additional interfunctional coordination as the new designs flowed through purchasing, material control, fabrication, assembly, and testing. The primary purpose of the groups was to supplement the formal hierarchy and provide a quick reaction capability to avoid damaging schedule disruptions as problems arose. One of the task forces was organized by major sections—wing, body, tail, etc. Another was organized by airplane number, that is, several men were assigned to each of the first six planes to be produced. Task force members worked full time for the task force as long as it existed.

The task forces were able to collect detailed and current information on an informal basis by walking through the plant and telephoning managers. This interfunctional information, which was not available anywhere else, gave them a basis for setting priorities as problems arose. Task force groups were also able to work with people who were most knowledgeable about the problem.

The task forces represented a temporary structure change which modified the authority relationship during periods of high uncertainty. During the period of new design introduction, the task force set priorities on what to do next. Since they had information which cut across functions and were not identified with any single function, the task force members were in a better position to determine priorities than were the functional managers. The functional managers still made decisions relating to who would do the work and how to do it. During periods of task certainty, the functional managers did not need priorities other than "follow the schedule!" But during a new model introduction, the assumptions on which the schedule was based often proved wrong, and the information collecting activities of the task force placed them in the position to set new priorities. Task forces generally disbanded after about six to ten planes had been built. (The task force organized around the airplane sections is a good example of the matrix organization.)

The 747 Program

The liaison group and the task force were limited in the degree of integration they could achieve. The liaison group was organized to link only two functions. The task force linked multiple functions but it was limited in the amount of information it could collect because it collected information by informal means. Since it was expensive to have managers devoting their time to seeking information, task force groups usually waited until a problem arose and collected information relevant to the problem. Since the task force was organized into self-contained units, such as a wing group, this further limited the amount of information they needed.

The use of liaison and task forces was not sufficient to cover the needs for additional coordination on the 747 program. The design was not highly preplanned and the problem was to integrate the design task as well as the manufacturing task. Due to less research and development the design parameters were not as complete as in prior programs. Thus when a problem arose there were many alternative solutions, and information was needed to estimate and evaluate the consequences of alternatives. With the reduced lead time design decisions had to be made without seriously disrupting the schedule. Of course activities could be rescheduled to facilitate the design task. These decisions placed considerable pressure on the decision-making apparatus.

An example of a hypothetical design problem can illustrate the magnitude of the decision problem. Suppose that the design group in systems was going to attempt a state of the art advance in the design of the actuator for the wing flaps.[15] It will operate hydraulically rather than electrically. This will increase its life, decrease its weight, and will take three months to develop. After two and a half months it appears that it will require another two months to complete the design. A decision is necessary. One class of alternatives would involve continuing with the state of the art advance and seek ways to put the actuator back on schedule by (1) using the remaining slack time and have manufacturing work overtime; (2) installing the device at a later date; (3) process design could design a faster and usually more expensive process to absorb the time; (4) instead of subcontracting the fabrication work, it could be produced internally to save time. The customer may be willing to accept a month's delay, but there are time and cost considerations attached to each of these alternatives.

A second class of alternatives would involve eliminating the state of the art advance and adopting a known actuator which could be

---

[15] The wing flaps are the movable portions of the wing which expand the size of the wing on take-off and landing. The larger wing area creates more lift for take-off and more drag for landing. A smaller wing is preferable for cruising.

operationalized in two weeks. However, the known actuator does not provide a weight saving and weight must be reduced some other way. Weight could be taken out of the airplane in other sections by using lighter but more expensive materials such as titanium for stainless steel or the engine producer might be able to increase the thrust of the engine. This means the weight could be tolerated without reducing performance targets on speed, range, and operating economy. Thus, there were multiple alternatives which required evaluation. The 747 product branch had to frequently handle such decision problems, and the alternative creation and consequence evaluation required inputs from all functions. Likewise, the final decision would require revision of task assignments, schedules, and budgets of all functions.

The general manager on the 747 had two alternative solutions to the design problem: (1) he could decentralize the decision-making, placing greater decision-making influence at the lower levels where the information existed, or, (2) he could bring the information up to the existing level of decision-making. The general manager on the 747 program chose the second alternative.

This was accomplished by making an organizational modification and by increasing the influence of the program manager's office. The organization of the product branch is shown in Figure 7.13. Other branches have recently followed by making similar changes in struc-

FIGURE 7.13

Product Branch Organization Responsible for 747

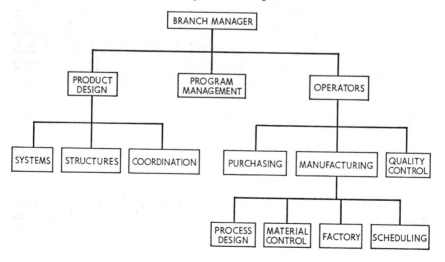

ture. This structure represents a more inclusive first-order grouping of the sequentially interdependent functions which took place after product design. The second-order grouping consisted of coupling the reciprocally interdependent design units with the sequentially interdependent operations functions. Also there was coupling with the division marketing group and major subcontractors. The incomplete preliminary design required substantial external interactions.

The other change was the increased influence of the program manager's office. This unit increased both the detail and the currency of the information displayed in the management control center. Previously detailed interfunctional information for decision-making had to be acquired informally by the task forces, but the new structure provided a more formal information system. The cost of the change was the large increase in clerical personnel to process the information.

More information does not necessarily result in better decisions unless there is an increase in the capacity to utilize it. For this purpose a PERT-like model of the design task was used.[16] These models display graphically the technological sequence of tasks to be performed, allowing the cause and effect relationships to be traced quite easily. Thus if there was a design problem, all subsequent tasks affected could be identified and those managers involved could be called to a meeting to decide what to do.

Thus the increase in task uncertainty and tighter coupling of functions was countered with more information and an increased decision-making capability. In the future as the uncertainty is decreased, however, the amount of information will be decreased. The frequency of reporting can be reduced from daily to weekly, weekly to bi-weekly. The PERT system will not be needed. The number of information processing people can be decreased to a normal level as the task certainty increases. Although the form of coordination is different, its intensity still varies directly with the uncertainty of the task.

Management by Anticipated Exception

The task force described earlier operated under the principle of management by exception. This conserved the amount of informa-

---

[16] For the original article describing PERT and its use on the Polaris program, see Donald Malcolm, John Roseboom, Charles E. Clark, and Willard Fazar, "Application of a Technique for Research and Development Program Evaluation," *Operations Research*, Vol. 7 (October, 1959).

tion that had to be collected. The 747 information system by contrast operated on the principle of management by anticipated exception. As the status of the program was updated periodically, potential problems were anticipated and resolved before they became real problems. Many were resolved by interfunctional teams or committees. Once a specific problem had been identified the functional personnel most familiar with the problem were assigned to a team to resolve it. The team existed until the problem was solved. All these teams were chaired by personnel of the program manager's office and made use of information in the control room. These teams differed from the task forces in that the members were not full-time team members. They were full-time functional personnel that periodically met until the problem was solved. There were several teams in action at any one time.

Change Boards

It is also interesting to contrast the committees and teams on the 747 with the change board committees, which represented two different committee strategies. The 747 program used the information system and PERT-like model to identify occasions for committee action, to create alternatives, and to assess and evaluate consequences.

The change board's activities were designed to eliminate the need for information. Instead of an information system it had elaborate classification schemes. Classification reduces the need for information by permitting much of the decision-making to be done prior to the need for it.[17] Thus the problem facing the change board was to distinguish the type of event and change some parameters in the predecided solution. The board was staffed by permanent representatives from each function who were trained in the appropriate classifications and responses. The price for this approach was that problem and solution did not match precisely. However, the problems were repetitive enough and small enough so that the costs of the mismatch outweighed costs of information collection and interaction to work out a solution for each problem individually. In addition, should a consequential problem arise, then additional effort could be brought to bear. Thus, problems were solved by applying a classification scheme and then a programmed decision for events of that class.

---

[17] March and Simon, op. cit., p. 163.

Events which were difficult to classify or consequential triggered an exception mechanism which conserved problem-solving effort.

The decision strategy of the 747 rejected this approach because their problems were consequential rather than repetitive.

Conclusions

The case study described in this paper has presented an organizational change following from an environmental change. In so doing the organization design problem was described by highlighting the alternative designs which were possible. Like many of the current writings in *Organization Theory*, this paper treated the predictability of the task as the basic independent variable influencing the design of the organization.[18]

The treatment of task predictability or uncertainty was different in this study as compared to the treatment by Lawrence and Lorsch. In this study uncertainty was considered as it affects the amount of information needed to coordinate interdependent departments. If the task is predictable, much of the activity can be preplanned, thereby eliminating the need for continuous communication. When the task is not understood before it is performed it requires additional information transmission; for example, if during the process of task performance it is discovered that schedules may be missed, more or less resources are needed, or designs require changing, this necessitates the adjustment of two or more departments. When the frequency of these events overloads the hierarchy, the organization must increase its ability to handle more information for coordination or reduce the need for coordination. The need for coordination can be reduced by altering the authority structure or by uncoupling the interdependent subunits with order backlogs and inventories. This case study showed how the sequence of activities at Boeing was originally uncoupled with slack time and inventories. However, the environmental change eliminated this alternative. The organizational response was to add coordination mechanisms to handle more information for coordination.

In contrast Lawrence and Lorsch treat the relative difference in uncertainty for interdependent subtasks in an organization. The

---

[18] Lawrence and Lorsch, *op. cit.*; Charles Perrow, "A Framework for the Comparative Analysis of Organizations," *American Sociological Review*, Vol. 32 (April, 1967); and Thompson, *op. cit.*

greater this difference in uncertainty the greater the differentation in attitudes and modes of operation. These differences, which are necessary for successful subtask performance, make subunit integration difficult. However, this is only a problem if the hierarchy cannot handle all the information processing. If it cannot, then coordination devices like direct contact, teams, and liaison men must be used. Thus the two approaches to using the concept of uncertainty are complimentary.

8 | Effective Management of Programs

James Burns

This article summarizes the findings of a study of program offices conducted by Burns at one of the leading firms specializing in doing advanced development work on a contract basis. Program offices are being increasingly turned to as an integrative procedure in technically complex organizations. Burns's analysis compares program offices that management selected as more effective with program offices that were selected as less effective. He examines the relationship between effectiveness and such factors as formal structure, office locations, role conceptions, and managerial orientations. He also examines the effect of the wider organizational setting on the work of the program offices. The implications of this study for some of the practical issues of managing such offices are spelled out. The entire study is reported in an unpublished doctoral dissertation submitted at the Harvard Business School entitled, "The Program Office, An Integrative Device." Burns is currently an assistant professor at the School of Business Administration at the University of Southern California.

CURRENTLY the Defense Department and NASA have several billions of dollars worth of contracted work which is being conducted by program organizations. Many firms in the consumer goods industry use similar systems, called product line management, to deal with a specific product or to work with a specific segment of the market. Specialization of this type has also occurred in the construction industry, which has developed project organizations to deal with tasks which are larger and more complex. Finally, when large organizations undertake jobs which are especially large or unique for the firm, they often use a technique called task management. Whatever their names, however, these systems are concerned with the effective management of programs.

Managing programs effectively is an especially critical issue today, particularly when we consider the probable future impact of this device upon management. Many authors have made projections about the organization of the future. Warren Bennis, for example, has given the following list of developments which will shape future organizations:

1. Rapid technological change and diversification will lead to inter-penetration of the government and legal and economic policies in business. Partnerships between government and business will be typical;
2. The general population will be characterized by increased edu-cation and job mobility;
3. People will be more intellectually committed to their jobs and will require more autonomy, involvement and participation in their jobs;
4. The task of the firm will be more technical, complicated, and unprogrammed; and,
5. The organization of the future will be an adaptive, rapidly changing, temporary system, which will be organized around problems to be solved.[1]

The list of organizational characteristics above very nearly de-scribes the program office presently being used in the aerospace indus-try. Certain key issues concerning program management are regularly discussed by people in program offices and by those individuals in resource groups who must service these program offices. Among the most important of these are:

What is the task of the program office?

What type and how much authority should the program manager have?

How should the program office be internally designed?

How does the program office achieve integration to accomplish its goals?

What are the characteristics of the wider organizational setting which facilitate effective operation of the program offices?

The Task of the Program Office

At first glance, people in a program office appear to be doing everything. Depending on the stage of the project, they may be involved in design, systems analysis and integration, production plan-ning, quality control, procurement, or any number of related tasks. It

---

[1] Warren G. Bennis, *Changing Organizations* (New York: McGraw-Hill Book Co., 1966), pp. 10–13.

could be argued that if these are the only tasks of the program office, then its existence cannot be justified, and it should be abolished. A functional department composed of systems analysts could develop a level of expertise which would make them much more effective in this area than part-timers in the program office. The same argument can be made about other functional specialists in the program office.

However, the primary task of the program office is the coordination of the work of others, so that the activities of the various functional groups can be integrated and the goals of the program accomplished. This may seem obvious, but many individuals within program offices do not see their job this way. They continue to see themselves as design engineers or quality control specialists—not as integrators. Nevertheless, if the task of the program office is integration, then there should be a direct connection between the degree of integration achieved and the performance of the program. Our research showed that this connection was valid: the better the integration achieved, the better the performance on the program task.

There are several understandable reasons for the fact that some program office personnel do not see themselves as integrators. When a program office runs into difficulty in integrating the activities of the necessary resource groups, there are two basic ways to overcome this integration difficulty. The office can concentrate its time and energy on improving the quality of integration, or, it can attempt to include within the program office individuals with the required resource skills, and thereby eliminate any need for integration. Since integration is not easily measured or accomplished, many managers select the second, apparently more direct alternative. This approach might be acceptable if it did not adversely affect the total organization.

The resource groups on which the program office depends are the primary subsystems of the total organization. In contrast to these resource groups the program office is more oriented to the short run. As the program office assimilates individuals who would normally be members of the resource groups, it shifts all of their attention to short-term problems. This shift reduces the strength of the resource groups, and in the long run is likely to hamper the effectiveness of the firm due to a lack of research, marketing, production, or other longer term skill development. Also, there are two other situations which may result from this approach. First, the program office is building skills which to a large extent are identical to those of a resource group, and this brings the two units into competition for certain types of work. This competition increases the conflict between the two groups, and can lead to an organization of openly hostile factions. Second, the task of the program office becomes much more complex. Whereas formerly the office specified *what* was required for the performance of a task, it now must also specify, for at least part of the program, *how* the task is to be performed. This additional work dilutes the impact of the office, and it may be forced into a position where it cannot concentrate on its primary responsibility. These possible adverse effects help to explain the finding of our research that the more effective program offices had a clearer perception of their primary task as being the achievement of integration.

Authority of the Program Manager

Many of the people who discuss program organization believe that operational problems are due to the program manager's having too little authority. They argue that the program manager must have full control over all the components of his program; he should be able to specify who does what, and when. This solution ignores the systematic complexity of the modern high technology firm. The firm may, at any one time, have a dozen or more programs in progress. Each of these will have a program manager, and each will draw on the same basic set of resource groups. It is impossible for each of these men to be independently specifying the "what" and "when" of his program. The resource groups must modify their schedules to service all of them. So the situation is not as simple as the generalization that the more authority any one program manager has, the more successful he will be in carrying out his program. In our research we attempted to clarify this relationship between authority and program effectiveness.

There were considerable differences in the levels of performance of the various programs we studied; in spite of this we determined that the various program managers possessed very similar amounts of authority. So it seemed that variables other than the amount of program manager authority were much more critical to a program's performance. In pursuing other variables we examined first the effect on the formal structural design of program offices and its effect on integration and performance.

Formal Structure of Program Offices

One of the most interesting questions asked by practitioners concerning program offices is, how can it be most efficiently designed to carry out its task? We have already said that the office must define its primary task as the achievement of integration. Our question then becomes, how can the office be designed to most effectively integrate the necessary resource groups to accomplish the program task? The answer seems somewhat obvious, but not trivial: Design the office with integration in mind.

In our study we observed two basic patterns for structuring the formal division of work within the program office. In the first pattern, the program office organized itself in terms of the physical parts or subsystems of the total product systems for which the group was responsible. For example, if the group was responsible for the development and manufacture of a small ground-to-ground missile, then subgroups such as propulsion systems, guidance systems, and propellant counter-measures would be established. We might call this a hardware-oriented structure.

The second type of organization structured itself quite differently —in terms of the key resource groups which it was required to integrate. For example, one of the program tasks was research and development skill, and so the program office developed an internal subgroup titled research and development. This group had the main responsibility for integrating the R & D effort. We would call this type of design a resource group structure.

Figure 8.1 shows the two types of program office organization and the types of integrative activity which they must carry out to do their task. Only three resource groups have been included in the diagram, but during the research we identified at least eleven critical resource groups. The reader can visualize the increasing organizational complexity under either arrangement as additional resource groups were added.

The figure also helps us visualize that any program office must deal with at least two levels of integration. If the program task is to be accomplished, the various resource groups must be integrated by the program office and, at the same time, the program office must develop methods or mechanisms by which it can integrate the efforts of its own members. We will deal with the first of these two tasks first.

In our study the more effective program offices used the resource group pattern of formal structure. These offices were organized so that individuals or subgroups had primary responsibility for the integration of one specific resource group. For example, three individuals in the program office might be assigned, as a subgroup, to integrate the

FIGURE 8.1

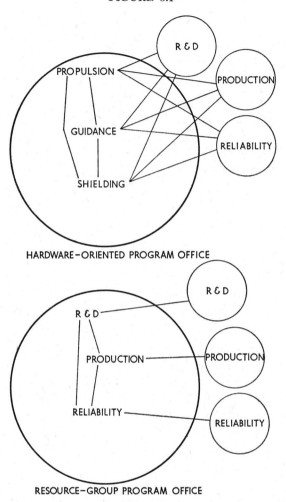

HARDWARE-ORIENTED PROGRAM OFFICE

RESOURCE-GROUP PROGRAM OFFICE

activities of the electronics design group with the program office. At the same time, because of the amount of work involved, only one man may be given the responsibility for integrating the activities of the procurement department with the program office.

Designing the program office in terms of its integrative task has several benefits. First, the individuals involved can better concentrate on developing relationships with people in a single resource group. This facilitates communication. They learn who to call and when, and they begin to find out who is a good source of information, and who can or will make decisions. Since formal organization charts for the resource groups do not really provide this information, regular informal contact seems to be the only answer. Second, these people develop a better understanding of the language system used by the resource groups. They learn what the abbreviations and slang of the group mean. They develop a deeper understanding of the problems faced by the resource groups and of the issues which interest them.

The chief problem with this type of organizational design is that by addressing itself almost entirely to the problem of integrating the resource groups with the office, the office tends to have difficulty achieving integration within itself. The individual who spends the bulk of his time working with an R & D group may become so interested and involved in their work that he forgets he is a member of the program office. However, we found that the program manager can personally handle the problem of integrating his own group more effectively than he can handle the resource group integration problem. Therefore, an organizational design which minimizes resource integration problems seems to be most appropriate. We will discuss some of the mechanisms for internal integration later.

Orientations for Integration with Resource Groups

We have described above one mechanism for achieving integration with resource groups: formal structure that places individuals in roles which induce concentration on the integrative task. In addition, in our study we examined other ways to accomplish the needed integration. Most of us have observed individuals who are extremely skillful as integrators or links between organizational units. Lawrence and Lorsch, in a recent article titled, "New Management Job: The Integrator," have listed and discussed certain characteristics and roles of these individuals. In our own research, however, we found that individual integrators, as such, did not exist in the program offices we examined. In most cases the program office had developed integrative subgroups. These groups had not been formally designed into the structure, but they had evolved over time as a need occurred. However, there were some interesting differences in the way they functioned. In the more effective offices, these subgroups had developed relationships with the resource groups which were of higher quality. Interactions were warmer and more open. Problems were freely discussed and both sides seemed to be working toward a sound and fair resolution. There seemed to be a great deal of empathy, and each side had a better understanding of the other.

In order to understand this process, we measured the differences in orientations and in the attitudes and feelings of the people involved which might affect these relationships. These people tended to have significantly different orientations which affected their day-to-day behavior. Three basic orientations which had been identified by Lawrence and Lorsch were used: Time, goal, and interpersonal orientation.

If the primary task of the program office is the integration of resource groups to complete the program task, then it follows that the program groups should have composite orientations which would be very close to a mean of the orientations of the resource groups. For example, production units tend to have very short time orientations —they are more concerned with day-to-day operations. Research groups, on the other hand, tend to be involved with more long-term activities, projects which would perhaps take several years to complete. If a program office had to integrate only the activities of a research group and a production group to do its task, we would expect the mean time orientation of the program office to be intermediate. Second, we would expect the program office subgroup which is working with the production unit to have a time orientation somewhere between the intermediate orientation of the program office as a whole and the very short time orientation of the production unit.

Our data showed that the first assumption was valid. The program offices did tend to have orientations which approximated the mean of the orientations of the resource groups. In addition the more closely each program office was able to approximate this mean, the more effective it was in carrying out its task, that is, the more balanced the office, the more able it was to meet its cost, schedule, and technical plans.

Our second assumption concerning the mid-point orientations of subgroups linking specific resource groups was also supported. In the program offices which had not been specifically defined for integrative activities, the relationship between these linking mid-point orientations and effective performance of the program task was especially significant. The more a program office was able to develop linking subgroups which had orientations between the program office and the resource groups, the more effective it was in completing its task.

Another factor of importance, as was pointed out above, is the achievement of integration within the program office. The activities of the members of the program office must be coordinated. A breakdown in the integration between members of the program office can be just as serious in its consequences as a lack of integration of resource units.

Integration within the Program Office Itself

The ability of any group of people to work together does not just happen. This is especially true of a unit like the program office, which is composed of people drawn from widely differing backgrounds and with substantial differences in interest. One variable which seems particularly critical to internal integration is the physical location of the program office. The most successful of the offices studied had all but two of its members physically located in one large office. There were no partitions and members talked back and forth continually.

The two members not located in this large office area had very specialized tasks which seemed to require little integration with the other elements of the task. It is interesting to note that these two isolates, according to our interpersonal orientation measure, had interpersonal styles which were considerably less open than those of other members of the office. It seemed that these men because of their personal characteristics had been given jobs and offices which permitted them to be loners. The program manager had a private office which was about ten feet from the large office area, but he made frequent trips in and out of this office area to ask questions and provide information. The amount of interaction, its duration and the range of its content, seemed to be higher in this program office than in the other offices studied.

The office which was considered the poorest performer had a different physical layout. All members of this program group had individual offices. The program manager's office was removed from the other offices and he seldom contacted individual program members. The laboratory was completely isolated from the office area. If an engineer wished to talk to someone in the lab, he either had to go to the lab or use the telephone. It was rare to see more than two individuals in a discussion at any one time, and there was substantially less social interaction. In summary, one office appeared to have been designed physically to facilitate interaction and a cohesive social structure which led to effective integration, while the other office appeared to have been physically designed to block interaction and prevent integration. (Actually, most program groups have office space which is somewhere between the two extremes.) The administrator should therefore be aware of the effect of the office layout on the performance of the program office.

Formal meetings, such as budget meetings and report meetings, also helped the program office to achieve internal integration. The most interesting and apparently the most useful type of meeting for aiding integration was the design review meeting. All members of the program office attended these meetings. In the process of making decisions on various design alternatives, all members of the program office said what they thought and made recommendations. But once a decision was reached, it became a group decision and everyone shared the responsibility for it. One program manager explained, "After a design review, no one can sit back and say I wouldn't have done it that way. Everyone had a chance to express their viewpoints and they were part of the decision. It really makes you feel more relaxed. You don't feel like you are out on a limb all alone."

This shared responsibility increased team spirit and helped in the resolution of disputes.

Finally, certain internal reporting systems may be used to record and transmit information. Generally, these devices do not really aid in the information transmission process, because all members have already heard this information. The recording function, however, does tend to force the members of the office to deal directly with the situation at some specific point in time and to reach some consensus on what the actual situation is and on the procedures to be followed in the future. It therefore prevents avoiding issues.

We cannot look at the program office and the effectiveness of its task performance without also saying something about the larger organizational context in which it operates. In the following section we shall talk about some of the general organizational elements which seem to facilitate program office task performance.

The Wider Organization Setting

Certain norms and beliefs, when held throughout the organization, seem to facilitate program performance. In describing these beliefs we will also be interested in looking at the mechanisms which assist their development and maintenance. While many of the following statements will seem self-evident most of us have seldom seen them as fully operational as in the organization under study.

Influence Based on Technical Knowledge. When individuals were interviewed and data were collected concerning the amount of influence held by members of the organization, it became clear that influence was not really a direct function of hierarchical position. Those individuals who had the greatest technical expertise were viewed as having the most influence. While technical ability was paramount, it was obvious that people in the firm also realized the importance of cost and schedule. The interesting way in which these three factors were interrelated in this firm is best explained by one of the program members who said: "Most of us in this company want to be able to work on interesting problems. We, of course, realize that to obtain interesting projects we have to meet schedules and live within our budget on current work." The members of the organization were willing to meet schedule and live within budget constraints, not because of any unique desire to see high corporate profits, but because they saw a connection between this and future desirable features in future assignments. The strong desire for technical excellence helped the firm solve problems of integration and also helped to establish an overall climate which most of the workers found very satisfying.

One of the most common integration problems faced by scientifically oriented firms is the inclusion of the ideas of the most advanced technical experts into the operation of programs. In many cases there is competition and even open hostility between these groups. This organization, in which influence was based on technical knowledge, was able to avoid this situation and to integrate the specialists at the appropriate time in program tasks. One program manager explained: "We continually inform the Corporate Program Development Group (a group of technical experts) about our progress on the program. It is essential that they be tapped for new ideas. Over 50% of all the creative ideas around here come from them."

The fact that technical skill determined the amount of influence a man had in the organization led most workers to believe that they were only limited in their progress in the firm by the rate of their technical development. This idea was further reinforced by certain management practices. One individual who held a job just below the professional engineering level described one of these practices:

You know, one thing about (the company) is that it is obvious if you develop your technical skills and become more proficient, you will get the promotions. They have a system here which fixes it so that even the lack of an engineering degree won't block your advancement to an engineering job. If you think you are ready, you can go before the board (a group of five senior level technical people) and be tested. If they find that you have sufficient technical ability you will be promoted to engineer. I don't know of any other company where this can happen.

This procedure allowed people without degrees to advance if they were competent. The board gave an extremely stiff examination, which might last as long as two days, and only the most qualified people could pass. This practice held out some hope for individuals who for one reason or another had not completed their formal education.

Non-evaluative Planning and Control Systems. Division management didn't use the formal planning and control systems to evaluate the performance of program personnel. The primary planning systems were the proposal itself and a PERT system. The proposal was developed by the program group. It was their plan and their estimate. Once it was formulated, submitted, and accepted, they felt committed to its successful completion. They did any replanning or re-estimating that was required. It was impossible to say later on that something had been imposed on them. The PERT system was used for detailed planning. Its main purpose was to ensure that the members of the program office were aware of all the elements of their task and the time constraints of each element. The PERT reports went to the program manager and were solely for his information. No one used the PERT system to evaluate or second guess his decisions or performance. The non-evaluative nature of these systems tended to lead to very accurate data, since there was no reason not to make them accurate. No one would be penalized for the data. Each program manager in this organization submitted a weekly report on the status of his program. It was his responsibility to identify problems and explain what he was doing about them. While there was no penalty for having a problem, individuals were severely reprimanded for trying to hide one. Many members of the organization expressed this norm in ways similar to the remarks below:

The one way you really get in trouble around here is to have a problem and hide it.

* * * *

One thing management just doesn't want is surprises. If they don't know about problems they can't help us solve them.

Conflict Should Be Confronted. The dominant means of resolving conflict in this organization was problem solving or confrontation.

Relevant issues and facts were placed on the table and openly discussed. The objective was to reach a solution best for the organization. If this method of resolving conflict did not work, a second method—forcing—was used. However, when data from this organization was compared to the data on other companies reported by Lawrence and Lorsch, it was found that confrontation was used to a greater extent than in any other company studied.

Conclusions

It seems clear that there is a direct relationship between the level of integration achieved by the program office, and the effective performance of its task. Practicing administrators must therefore concern themselves with how high levels of integration may be achieved.

The first and most important factor in the achievement of integration is the definition of the task of the program office. The members of the office must view their primary task and responsibility as being the achievement of integration. If they see their work in terms of engineering, research, or systems analysis, the integration effort will suffer and performance will be reduced. A second factor important to the accomplishment of integration is the way in which the office is internally structured. Offices which are specifically designed in terms of their integrative task, that is, by resource groups, tend to outperform offices with other types of structure. However, if the members of the program office form subgroups to work with resource groups, they can effectively achieve integration regardless of their formal organizational design. The parallel problem of achieving integration within the program office is facilitated by appropriate arrangements of physical space, by appropriate meetings, and reporting systems.

One final point which should be emphasized is the quality of the larger organization setting in which the program office exists. The program office does not exist in a vacuum. The characteristics of the organization in which it exists have a substantial impact on its performance. In this research, three basic features of the organization seemed to be especially important for the support of the program offices: Influence in the organization was very much dependent on technical knowledge and skill; the planning and control systems were non-evaluative in nature, with their primary purpose being to provide information to those who were responsible for decision-making; finally, the dominant mode of conflict resolution was confrontation.

9 | Entrepreneurship and Moderation: The Role of the Integrator

Dalmar Fisher

In this study of product managers in a consumer products company, Fisher has examined the problems of playing integrating roles in a large organization. His research, which represents his doctoral thesis at the Harvard Business School, has important management implications. What are the demands of these integrating positions? What sorts of persons will be effective integrators? What formal training might be helpful to develop effectiveness in these positions? Fisher answers these questions himself, but the research findings themselves may suggest additional answers to the reader, given the requirements of his own organization. Fisher is an assistant professor at Boston College.

How does it feel to be an integrator? Can we specify the demands of this new (or at least newly discovered) kind of managerial role? Or should we say simply that the integrator is an intuitive wizard, capable of performing in all ways toward all men at all times? Perhaps the job defies specific description. What discretion does he have? Or are his "hands tied," as some commentators have claimed? Again, can we begin to describe what the integrator must do in order to be effective?

These questions are important ones for at least two reasons. First, increasing technical specialization of the separate departments and units within organizations makes emphatic the need for coordination of effort. Secondly, complexities of markets and accompanying complication of organizational goals have resulted in increasing use of "matrix" structure, where one organization is, concurrently, several organizations. Here the traditional organization, with its marketing, research and production subunits, has superimposed upon it several project organizations, cutting across functional lines, each responsible

153

for one of the firm's several projects or products. It is the integrator, in this case the product or project manager, who faces much of the burden for making the "matrix" system work.

An increase can be expected in the number of managers who are given this responsibility for the integration of a project as opposed to the more traditional authority to direct subordinates. Lawrence and Lorsch have put it this way:

> One of the critical organizational innovations will be the establishment of management positions, and even formal departments, charged with the task of achieving integration. Moreover, the integrative function will be on a par with such traditional functions as production, sales, research and others.[1]

So many crucial decisions must be made in organizations today that the regular line hierarchy route for decision-making no longer works. Also, the new emphasis on research implies greater numbers of scientists in industry. The different personalities and working styles of these specialists add another dimension to the integration problem, since collaboration between people in different functions is essential. So the integrating job has become more complex as it has become more important. Lawrence and Lorsch describe the integrator's job as follows:

> The integrator's role involves handling the nonroutine, unprogrammed problems that arise among the traditional functions as each strives to do its own job. It involves resolving interdepartmental conflicts and facilitating decisions, including not only such major decisions as large capital investment but also the thousands of smaller ones regarding product features, quality standards, output, cost targets, schedules, and so on. . . . In recent years there has been a rapid proliferation of such roles as product manager, brand manager, program coordinator, project leader, business manager, planning director, systems designer, task force chairman, and so forth. The fine print in the descriptions of these various management positions almost invariably describes the core function as that of integration.[2]

Although the need for the integrator role seems clear, its effective implementation has been less well understood. In fact, both the specific demands of the job and the managerial behavior that is effective in coping with them have been the subjects of controversy.

---

[1] P. R. Lawrence and J. W. Lorsch, "New Management Job: The Integrator," *Harvard Business Review*, November–December, 1967, p. 142.
[2] *Ibid.*

CONTRARY VIEWS OF THE INTEGRATOR

Popular debate has centered around three questions: Whether or not the integrator has any real authority in the organization; Whether the requisites of his job can be specified; and Whether a certain kind of behavior style makes an individual integrator effective. First, on the question of authority, one view is that the integrator, by virtue of his cross-functional perspective, is truly the boss, since he "has all the required elements of command over all the resources he needs."[3] Quite opposite to this notion is the view that his hands are tied, since he has no line authority:

Management only nominally delegates authority to the product manager, and actually wants to maintain an active part in every decision.[4]

*   *   *   *

We have observed that product managers tend to be fettered by organizationally imposed constaints which hinder or preclude their effective action.[5]

*   *   *   *

Product managers have no real authority.[6]

On the matter of specifying the integrator's job, it has been suggested, on the one hand, that this is impossible, because every integrator's job is unique: "Both his authority and his set of relationships will be different in every situation. . . . What he does and how he works should depend entirely on the requirements of the particular product and its markets."[7]

An alternate suggestion is that the variations between different integrator's jobs are not infinite, but rather are determined by the nature of the particular departments within the organization with which he must work.[8] This research-based opinion is consistent with a

---

[3] James E. Webb (Administrator, National Aeronautics and Space Administration), "New Challenges for Organization," *Harvard Business School Bulletin*, March–April, 1967, p. 13.

[4] Comment by a product manager in the food industry. Y. Roscow, "Product Managers: Just What Do They Do?" *Printers' Ink*, October 28, 1966, p. 13.

[5] D. J. Luck and T. Nowak, "Product Management: Vision Unfulfilled," *Harvard Business Review*, May–June, 1965, p. 143.

[6] David North of David North Associates in "Product Manager Cuts Companies' Flexibility," *Advertising Age*, May 15, 1967, p. 1.

[7] B. C. Ames, "Payoff from Product Management," *Harvard Business Review*, November–December, 1963, p. 141.

[8] P. R. Lawrence and J. W. Lorsch, "Differentiation and Integration in Complex Organizations," *Administrative Science Quarterly*, June, 1967, p. 1.

popular view, frequently expressed, that a major determinant of the integrator's results is the quality of his interpersonal relationships. For example, one practitioner has urged that "to the extent that the product manager can solicit cooperation from other departments, his scope is unlimited."[9]

Finally, concerning the individual qualities that make for effective integrator performance, some commentators lament that we simply do not know: "What sort of people do we need to manage and carry out this kind of effort? What qualities identify the individual with this type of temperament and capability? How do we go about developing such people to fill their potential? Very little is known about this. It is all too new. . . . This may well be the greatest challenge.[10]

On the other hand, two research reports have indicated that there are certain particular personal characteristics associated with integrator effectiveness. Among these were technical knowledgeability, a balanced or inter-departmental point of view, willingness to confront conflicts, a high need for affiliation with people combined with moderate achievement and power motives and a strong preference for taking the initiative and assuming leadership.[11]

A RESEARCH-BASED VIEW

Despite their seeming opposition to one another, these viewpoints made valuable contributions to our design of a research study focusing on twenty-three integrators, the members of the product management department of a large food products firm.[12] The particular need for product managers (or brand managers, as they are often called in other organizations) in companies such as the one studied has re-

[9] John D. Twiname, Marketing Manager of American Hospital Supply, a division of American Hospital Supply Corporation, in G. H. Evans, *The Product Manager's Job* (New York: American Management Association, 1964), p. 20.

[10] Webb, *op. cit.*, p. 15.

[11] Lawrence and Lorsch, "New Management Job: The Integrator," *op. cit.* G. H. Litwin and A. Siebrecht, "Integrators and Entrepreneurs," *Hospital Progress*, September, 1967.

[12] This study, to be discussed in the remainder of this chapter, was reported in the author's doctoral dissertation, "The Appraisal of Performance in the Product Management Function," Harvard Graduate School of Business Administration, 1968. The thesis was supervised by Associate Professor David Moment, Professor Louis B. Barnes and Associate Professor Jay W. Lorsch, all of Harvard Business School, and was supported in part by The Center for Research in Careers, Harvard Graduate School of Education, under the sponsorship of the National Institute of Mental Health. A more detailed account of this study will be reported in a forthcoming book by David Moment and Dalmar Fisher, *Roles, Styles and Effectiveness* (Boston: Division of Research, Harvard Graduate School of Business Administration, in preparation).

sulted from two powerful trends, the increasing number of products being produced and marketed by a particular organization, and the increasing degree of specialization within organizations. In large multi-product companies the attention given to each product must be balanced and coordinated as it moves through the various functions, especially manufacturing, marketing, and sales. The product manager does this planning, so that individual products receive proper attention from each department. Furthermore, because the men working within the various functions have become more and more specialized, an important part of the product manager's job is to coordinate the efforts of these specialists as an individual product passes through the various functional departments.

As suggested earlier, our interest was in the immediate pressures confronting the integrator, the product manager in our study, and in the options he exercised in response to these pressures.

Identifying the Demands

We have noted a lack of consensus about the formal requirements of the integrator's job as well as the absence of agreed-upon informal traditions concerning this new managerial role. We felt, therefore, that our subjects' job demands could best be specified in terms of the actual expectations of each product manager's immediate work associates. Our research design included interviews with the product managers about their relationships with their work colleagues and interviews with a number of other managers, including our subjects' superiors and subordinates within the product department as well as managers from other functional areas and from the company's advertising agencies, who worked closely with the product managers.

In addition, we developed a way of measuring expectations by means of a questionnaire survey. In our questionnaires we asked the colleagues of each product manager (PM) to describe that particular product manager's behavior using two instruments. These were Harrison and Oshry's *Organizational Behavior Description Survey* (OBDS) and a modified version of the Gough *Adjective Check List* (ACL).[13] We also asked each colleague for a scale rating of the productivity of his work relationship with the product manager he had

[13] R. Harrison and B. I. Oshry, "The Impact of Laboratory Training on Organizational Behavior," unpublished paper, 1967. H. G. Gough, *The Adjective Check List* (Palo Alto, Calif.: Consulting Psychologists Press, 1952). Our modification of the ACL contained words from the Achievement, Order, Autonomy and Affiliation scales developed by A. B. Heilbrun at the State University of Iowa.

described. These data allowed us to measure colleague expectations by comparing the ways colleagues described product managers with whom they said their work relationships were highly productive with the ways they described those with whom they reported less-productive relationships. We will discuss later how this analysis, along with our interview data, helped us account for much of the disagreement concerning the product manager's job. We discovered that the colleagues' expectations differed, not randomly, but rather depending upon the part of the organization structure where the colleague's own job was located.

To determine who the particular colleagues were who worked closely with each product manager, we asked each PM to list for us the names of his six to eight most important work associates, regardless of whether they were located inside the product department, in other parts of the company, or outside the company. We recognized in this way that each product manager's job was in some ways unique and self-determined. A numerical coding system was developed for completed questionnaires, so that all responses would be anonymous.

Identifying Coping Styles

Beyond gathering data about PM-colleague relationships, we also collected interview and questionnaire data from each product manager on his own view of his work behavior, the priorities he attached to certain components of his job and on certain of his underlying thought patterns. These data allowed us to compare product managers with each other. We found that product managers who were seen by their colleagues as relatively successful in fulfilling the colleagues' diverse and often conflicting expectations had certain personal characteristics that differed substantially from those of the less successful product managers. In other words, product managers who more effectively met the different demands they encountered from different sectors of the organization had coping styles unlike those employed by their less effective counterparts.

UNIVERSAL COLLEAGUE EXPECTATIONS

Colleagues from different organizational locations were not entirely in disagreement with one another. On two of our questionnaire measures, colleagues from all areas expressed similar preferences concerning product manager behavior. These were rational-technical competence and verbal dominance. Nearly all colleagues expected the PM to exhibit these two qualities. Again, we were able to infer this expectation from the fact that, in general, colleagues gave higher scores on these scales to their preferred product managers than they did to those with whom they reported less productive work relationships. This result confirmed the earlier research findings relative to the importance of leadership and technical competence in the integrator role. In the present study, colleagues' ratings on rational-technical competence and verbal dominance were highly correlated with each other, indicating that in the integrative function technical competence must be expressed through verbal dominance.

However, our results were not as simple as they at first appeared, for we also found an almost complete absence of agreement between colleagues from different organizational areas as to just which product managers were the ones who were most skillful at forming productive work relationships. Apparently, therefore, technical competence and verbal dominance meant different things to different colleagues. As we have already suggested, our data resolved this anomoly by revealing that the behavioral components of product manager productivity depended upon the organizational position *from* which the product manager was viewed.

ORGANIZATIONALLY RELATED EXPECTATIONS

Task Expectations

Our interviews indicated that product managers worked closely with two categories of colleagues from outside the product department whose jobs differed importantly from one another. The first group, which we termed his External-Professional colleagues, held jobs oriented mainly toward the firm's external environment or toward a professional reference group. The External-Professionals consisted of advertising agency personnel and members of the company's market research, product research, sales and legal departments. We referred to the second grouping as the product manager's Internal-Institutional colleagues. This grouping included managers in the company's accounting, manufacturing, purchasing, home economics, and promotion administration departments. In contrast to the External-Professionals, whose jobs involved attempts to change the firm in small, and sometimes larger ways, in order to adapt it to its competitive, technological and social environments, the Internal-Institutionals were more dominantly concerned with stabilizing and maintaining the firm's internal systems and procedures.

Consistent with this difference in orientation stemming from their differing functions in the organization, these two colleague groupings expected different task orientations of the product manager. The External-Professionals wanted to move product managers in the direction of greater entrepreneurship and innovative experimentation. For example, product managers frequently mentioned cases where their advertising agency colleagues had tried to move a bit too fast or too far with a new idea. One mentioned a situation where the agency recommended immediate national distribution of three new flavors on his brand, adding that he had to disapprove in favor of additional test marketing. Another described an agency recommendation for departure from established copy strategy involving inclusion of exotic foreign recipes in a newspaper ad. The product manager felt it more important to stress the product's ease of preparation. One agency account executive stated his preferences in this way: "It is a matter of literalness versus non-literalness; that's where all the debate is. The PM is very concerned with the explicitness with which things are stated. We are more concerned with communicating it in a way that it will be provocative and interesting."

One of the company's sales managers voiced his preference for entrepreneurial departure in the following manner:

> What I generally will want from the product department is greater quantities on promotional deals. They will say, "There's not enough money for that. If you can sell that much at two cents off, why not try selling it at regular?" Most of the time I'll have to say, "You're giving us too damn little." But just enough of the time I'll say, "Ample; just right," and in this way I'm able to maintain their respect.

The Internal-Institutionals, on the other hand, wanted product managers to direct their brands in a more moderate, less entrepreneurial way. One manufacturing manager, for example, objected to a product manager's request for new quality control procedures on his brand:

PRODUCT MANAGER: I've been asked about this: what are we going to do to assure taste? I'm expected to know exactly what you are going to do on this product.

MANUFACTURING MANAGER: But we *know* how to do quality control. What's the matter, don't you trust us? We'll use the same techniques on this product that we do on other products having similar ingredients.

In a similarly moderate vein, an accountant had this to say:

It's the nature of the PM to be optimistic. Our nature is to be a little more conservative on costs. Right now I'm working on a project. The idea is to try to show that sometimes more is spent on test marketing than is justified. Naturally, the product department wants to spend as much as possible in test market to make it look good. And the company is, as you know, strongly market-oriented. There's going to be a tendency for things to go the way of the marketing point of view.

The product manager's colleagues within the product department, his superiors and his subordinates, also expressed differing views about moderation and entrepreneurship. One superior discussed his preference for innovativeness:

We have in the group of young new people we've brought in here a group you would have to call some of the brightest young guys in the country. So then what happens to them? They spend the next two years learning the standard procedures and learning the system. Sure, they have to learn these things about the company, but what worries me is what happens to their creativity in the process. What you get is two types of product managers, loose and un-loose. The latter walk around with a book under their arm. That's how you can identify them. In the book are all their follow-ups: "Call this guy to check on this and this, etc."

The product managers' subordinates admired innovative behavior by their bosses, but also expected stability in the form of a certain amount of guidance and task structuring. In a typical comment, a subordinate noted the difficulties of working under excessively non-directive supervision: "There are risks in his being sort of detached from your work and saying, 'Come in and see me only when you have problems,' because then you're only working with him when you have problems instead of when you're trying to generate opportunities."

Our interview data were confirmed by colleagues' responses to the questionnaires. External-Professionals and Superiors selected adjectives connoting entrepreneurship (*adventurous, individualistic, daring, opportunistic, unconventional*) to describe those product managers with whom they reported highly productive relationships. Internal-Institutionals selected adjectives connoting moderation (*conventional, cautious, moderate, contented, conservative*). Subordinates indicated on their questionnaires a mild preference for both entrepreneurship and moderation.

Social-Emotional Expectations

Colleagues expected more from the product managers with whom they worked than just particular orientations toward the task. They expected certain social-emotional performances as well. The following comments by two External-Professionals, an agency executive and a market research manager, are illustrative:

> Sometimes they will seem to be always stopping everything we recommend. But I work with one PM who is not this way. He is a gutsy, and I think a very knowledgeable guy. He will say, "It may be my ass, but I am going to take a chance and try to get it through the guys upstairs."

> *   *   *   *

> The thing I think varies is the intrinsic confidence they have in their own ability. Sometimes I hear one of them talking and I have the clear feeling that what I am hearing is somebody up the line talking, and furthermore, that the guy who is standing in front of me doesn't have the words of the guy up the line he heard it from exactly straight.

The External-Professionals wanted the PM to express his beliefs openly and vigorously. To their preferred product managers they gave high ratings on a questionnaire scale entitled "Emotional Expressiveness," containing such items as *He tends to be emotional* and *You can tell quickly when he likes or dislikes what others do or say.* Thus our data strongly refuted the notion of some critics that business organizations are places where only conventional and inhibited behaviors are tolerated. The External-Professionals confronted the product manager with a demand for open interchange and fast, candid feedback.

The Internal-Institutionals expected quite different behavior. They did not want the PM to give full vent to his feelings. They preferred product managers whom they rated relatively low on the *Emotional Expressiveness* scale and whom they described using adjectives such as *deliberate, methodical* and *steady*, connoting a preference for emotional regulation and orderliness. In addition, they demanded warm acceptance and trust. Typical remarks made by Internal-Institutionals to the product manager associates were, "Don't destroy our whole structure," "Don't annoy our people," and, as we heard earlier, "What's the matter, don't you trust us?"

The product manager's Superiors expected still another social-emotional performance. Their preference was for an assertive, rather aggressively dominant style. They rated as most productive their relationships with product managers whom they saw as relatively low on consideration and warmth and suggested to the PM that he deal with his other colleagues by "telling them, not asking them." As one PM, involved in discussions with the cost accountants, was advised by his boss: "You've got to get tough with these guys. They want to make the estimates very conservative so they will look good later. This isn't chemistry. Formulas will carry you only part of the way. There comes a point where you have to get behind one alternative and *charge!*"

Finally, the product manager's Subordinates, as noted earlier, wanted the PM to provide them with a certain amount of structured guidance. But they also wanted him to relax occasionally his rigor and formality. Subordinates described their most productive relationships as being with product managers who were *appreciative, impulsive, talkative,* and *leisurely.* In other words, Subordinates wanted to be included on informal, as well as formal occasions. One Subordinate regretted that he did not have this sort of relationship with his PM:

Generally, things coming down to me from above follow channels fairly closely. It's never been a matter where he'd say, "Let's get together and decide." I think I have a very formal relationship with him. In some cases a guy can have a very strong formal relationship and also a very strong informal relationship. I don't think I have a very strong informal relationship with my boss.

Subordinates, as a group, used the adjectives *cynical* and *obliging* to describe product managers with whom they reported relatively low-productive relationships. They wanted their bosses' behavior toward them to be genuine. They were no more interested in being told that they were on their own and had to "produce or else" than they were in being patronized.

Summary: The Demand for Differentiated Behavior

To recapitulate, we found that the inability of colleagues from different locations in the organization to agree on which product managers were most productive was not a random happening. Rather, they disagreed because the disparate natures of their own jobs made it appropriate for them to expect different things of the PM. Organizationally different colleagues differed, first, in the task orientations they preferred the product manager to have. They also differed in the social-emotional performances they expected of him. Our twenty-three integrators, then, were faced with four distinct sets of expectations that differed because of the particular organizational locations from which they came. These four sets of expectations, along with their organizational sources, are summarized in Table 9.1.

This table implies that the integrator, if he is to be seen as effective by many or all of his key associates, must be seen differently by different associates. More specifically, he must vary his behavior depending upon the particular sector of the organization with which he is working at a given time. Given the discrepancies between the four sets of expectations, we can suggest that the integrator would do well,

TABLE 9.1

Behaviors Expected of the Product Manager
and their Organizational Sources

Organizational Source	Expectations Concerning Task Orientation	Expectations Concerning Social-Emotional Style
External-Professional	Entrepreneurship	Open expressiveness, high rate of interchange
Internal-Institutional	Moderation	Trust, restriction of emotionality, orderliness
Superiors	Entrepreneurship	Assertion and dominance
Subordinates	Entrepreneurship and moderation	Genuine inclusion

where possible, to meet with colleagues from different sectors at different times rather than simultaneously. During our observations in the food products firm it seemed that the product managers' more productive meetings were those where representatives of only one colleague grouping were present.

But just what sort of an individual is the integrator who succeeds in working productively with these diverse colleagues? From our discussion so far it might be reasoned that he has to be whatever other people want him to be; that he must be all things to all men. We found, however, that this was decidedly not the case.

THE HIGH PERFORMING INTEGRATOR

Our questionnaire data allowed us to make a comparison between integrators who were rated as high performers by their colleagues and those who were seen as relatively less effective. We considered a product manager to be a high performer if he was described, by colleagues from two or more of the four colleague groups, as tending to fulfill their groups' expectations in terms of the ACL words and OBDS items they used to describe him. Compared with the others, the high performers were apparently more nearly fulfilling the general requirement of the integrator role, that of working productively with organizationally diverse associates.

While they managed to fulfill conflicting expectations, the high performers were anything but conciliatory. In fact, their most distinguishing characteristic was their tendency to take an assertive position. As one high-performing product manager described it: "I think one of the over-riding things that characterizes the successful guy around here is his ability to inject himself into the projects and solutions of problems that confront his brands. In other words, it's a personal thrust that starts the fires burning in every functional area."

Another high performer, discussing his relationship with his superior, noted that if he disagreed with his boss he would ". . . fight him on it. On the other hand, he is a guy who has progressed, and he's obviously done so because of good thinking, so why not make his thinking part of your own thinking. You try and pick up what he has done and contribute your own thoughts to it."

The assertiveness of the high performers, then, was not blind thrust. It included attending to and internalizing the valid contributions of their colleagues. In describing themselves on their questionnaires, the high performers used words connoting both assertive autonomy and systematic orderliness with significantly greater frequency than did the others. Conversely, the lower rated product managers described themselves with words connoting passivity.[14] In an interview, one of the latter group discussed his less initiatory, more reactive approach to working with colleagues: "I didn't like *telling* them. I will go and say, 'Here's our problem; what can you recommend?' With the agency, for example, I guess I get as many projects *from* them as I give *to* them to do."

The high performers had a keen interest in the process of setting

---

[14] In describing themselves on the Adjective Check List, the high performers checked the words *ambitious, unconventional, opportunistic, self-confident, organized, alert, logical, reliable* and *precise* with significantly greater frequency than did the low performers. The low performers tended to describe themselves as *relaxed, easygoing, contented, conventional, leisurely.*

strategic goals for their brands. On one group of questionnaire items, each PM was asked to rate the importance of several specific tasks involved in product management. In every case where the task item had to do with formulating overall goals and strategy, the high performers rated the task as more important than did their lower-performing counterparts. Here again our data were suggesting that the integrator must take an assertive stand, giving his colleagues something upon which to bring their specialties to bear. In a similar vein, but at the level of more underlying personality characteristics, the high performers scored significantly higher on a test of independence of judgment, designed to measure the individual's ability to reach his own conclusions in the face of coercive pressure from other people.[15]

Despite the conflicting pressures of their jobs and their lack of traditional line authority, it obviously did not seem to the high performers that their hands were tied. Compared with the others, they reported a greater feeling of capability for handling added responsibility, less of a feeling that they were working under pressure in their jobs and less disagreement with company policies. Furthermore, they described themselves as more effective in every instance on several questionnaire items asking them to rate their own performance. In other words, the high performers expressed greater self-esteem and felt more confident and comfortable in their jobs. The lower-performing group thought less of themselves and felt more put upon by their surroundings. These findings clearly suggest that the integrator who does not take assertive, positive action will find himself rather painfully acted-upon.

TOWARD MORE EFFECTIVE PERFORMANCE

Our research results carry implications for integrators themselves as well as for those who manage integrators. We have seen that the effective integrator needs to view himself as an active leader rather than a passive coordinator. In doing so, he must be acutely aware of the interpersonal context of his job. One of our product managers said, "My problems are business problems." They are not that exclusively. His problems are social and emotional problems as well. Furthermore, he must be aware of the *four different* social-emotional-

---

[15] This test, developed by Frank Barron, is described in his article "Some Personality Correlates of Independence of Judgment," *Journal of Personality*, Vol. 21 (1953), p. 287–97.

business contexts in which he works. Since his four kinds of colleagues are diversely motivated, he must, in effect, "segment his own market" inside the organization as well as his product's market outside.

For those who manage integrators, how can more effective performers be recruited and developed? On the first matter, recruits need to be made more adequately aware of the multiple demands of the job. Many of them subsequently go out rather than up, not because they are incompetent, but because they expected and wanted the job to be either more exclusively enterepreneurial or more stable and structured than it turned out to be.

For the development of present and prospective integrators, training experiences are needed that more fully simulate the demands of the job. The current state of the art of management training, including techniques such as in-basket cases, role-playing exercises, and dialogues with the computer, clearly permits this, though specific tailoring of these tools is called for. For training integrators, a dialogue with four computer terminals, rather than just one, seems relevant. Still more appropriate might be the newly emerging educational techniques employing multimedia materials. The effective integrator appears able to receive messages via a rather noisy four-track sound system and, simultaneously, by other means as well.

The major point, however, is the need for greater awareness. Regardless of how many tapes or terminals may be involved, an increase in the ratio of knowledge to intuition is needed on the part of those responsible for the integrative function.

10 | Planning as Integration

Mrityunjay Athreya

This chapter presents highlights from Athreya's unpublished doctoral dissertation, "Guidelines for the Effectiveness of the Long Range Planning Process," Harvard Business School. As he indicates, there is a growing management interest in formal long-range planning. Athreya has studied four different planning offices with different reputations for effectiveness. These offices are operating in firms coping with different environmental conditions. He has focused on the *process*, as distinct from the content, of planning and has discovered a number of factors that bear on the results of the process. He has found it useful to conceive of the planning office as a mechanism to help achieve integration between the differentiated major departments of the enterprise. While overall planning must remain in the last analysis a general management responsibility, this study does provide some useful guides for making planning offices an important adjunct to the planning effort. Athreya is now on the faculty of the Indian Institute of Management, Calcutta.

ALL writers on management, from classical theorists to contemporary writers, have spoken of "planning" as an integral part of the role of managements of formal organizations. In fact, the existence of many successful businesses is at least partial after-the-fact evidence that they have had some form of planning. Effective planning in particular seems to be a major contributing element in the survival and success of businesses in a consumer-based, competitive environment.

While the term planning can refer to such short-term activities as preparing next week's production schedule, we are more concerned here in planning for a much longer time horizon, involving questions of corporate strategy, structure, and development. Formal planning as a routine activity is something of a recent phenomenon in organizations, but it is rapidly coming into vogue. More and more corporations are setting up formal Planning Departments. Why is this happening? There are many explanations. Part of this phenomenon is perhaps due to the "demonstration" effect. Another explanation might be that formalized planning represents an attempt on the part of corporations to cope with increasingly diverse and expanding environments.

To say that business units are operating in more complex environments is a statement of fact. Complexity is already so great that we can no longer speak of a business' environment, but should instead talk about the various subenvironments. These subenvironments are typically the environments facing the functional subsystems of a business. For example, Lawrence and Lorsch in their study of differentiation and integration have looked at organizations as having three major subsystems and corresponding subenvironments: marketing, technoeconomic, and scientific.

Another fact of organizational existence is the division of labor. Historically, businesses have evolved through various stages, from the owner-manager one-man-show, to a family group, to a functional organization, and finally to a divisionalized set-up with product and geographic decentralization. In an attempt to cope adequately with an expanding environment, businesses used division of labor as a strategy to permit the subsystems to cope with their particular subenvironments. But in the process the subsystems tend to develop certain characteristics not necessarily shared by the other subsystems, such as structure, time, values, and goal orientations. For instance, the hierarchy and lines of command in the factory or the regional sales office are often more pronounced than in R and D. Similarly, the scientist in the R & D department may have a time perspective that stretches into the next five years and beyond, while the engineer on the shop floor may be most concerned with the current week's production targets, and the salesman with the current week's sales quota. Such segmentation and development of unique characteristics by the subsystems is defined as *differentiation*.[1]

From the point of view of the organization as a whole, differentiation is a mixed blessing. Subsystems may become so wrapped up in their own interests that the organization's overall interests are ignored. Subsystems must somehow be kept in step in order to achieve unity of effort. This process of bringing together the efforts of the

---

[1] The definitions given here for differentiation and integration are consistent with those given by Lawrence and Lorsch.

subsystems in order to achieve the organization's total task is defined as *integration*.[2]

On balance, differentiation and integration can be very functional to an organization. It follows that the problems of integration cannot be solved by stifling differentiation, when differentiation is necessary due to the diversity of the environment. The operational question then becomes: How do you achieve integration most effectively?

The Emergence of the Planning Department

Given the emergence of planning departments at the corporate and divisional levels in the last decade, it seems plausible that these planning departments are integrative devices emanating from the need for integration in growing businesses with product and geographical diversification. This seems plausible for the following reasons: In the early stages of business organization, as in organizations in other facets of society, a sense of direction was imparted by the "leader," by virtue of his intimate knowledge of all relevant facts, and charisma. At a later stage a caucus of top managers performed this function. But a consequence of the greater environmental diversity and subsystem differentiation is that a small group of people at the apex of the organization have neither the time nor the competence to be intimately conversant with the subsystem requirements, and to bring about coordination. As a result, responsibilities for coordination are delegated, much like the earlier delegation of functional responsibilities. This delegation takes various forms. First, there is delegation down the hierarchy. Second, part of the burden of coordination is taken by what have come to be called management control systems, incorporating the concepts of performance measurement and reward-punishment structures. Both, while useful, have proved insufficient. At some stage, committees called by various names spring up in response to the need for integration. Such initially ad hoc devices gradually become formalized into what Lawrence and Lorsch call "integrative devices."

Realizing the growing need for coordination in large corporations, and being aware of the increasing number of planning departments to appear, we sought to further explore these developments in a study of the process of long-range planning. We intended to discover how the

---

[2]*Ibid.*

planning process contributes to effective integration by focusing on the organizational and behavioral aspects of the interaction between the planning and operating subsystems. In addition, we hoped to learn which particular characteristics and practices of planning departments made them most successful as integrative devices.

The research was conducted in two large corporations, by means of interviews, questionnaires, and examination of various corporate documents. A more detailed discussion of our research follows.

Nature of the Study

As we observed earlier, formal planning departments are a recent phenomenon, and there is as yet no generally accepted definition of long-range planning. We found the following definition useful for our purposes:

Long-range planning is a formal program under which an individual designated as director of planning or by a similar title, usually with a staff, is given the responsibility to ensure that the subsystems within the organization prepare coordinated plans for the long-range (usually three years and beyond.)

Our study was concerned with the *process* of long-range planning, as opposed to its substance—that is, the content of the plan itself. Recognizing the central role of the planner in the planning process, our principal research question became, "what are some of the important attributes and skills of the planner that are related to the effectiveness of the long-range planning process?"

Earlier we stated our hypothesis that the planning department is an integrative device evolving as part of the coping response of organizations to complex environments. Keeping this in mind, as well as the insights of the differentiation-integration model, the following detailed hypotheses were derived:

The long-range planning process is likely to be more effective to the extent that the planner possesses the following attributes and skills.
1. His position in terms of time, task and interpersonal orientations is intermediate between those of the various line and staff managers.
2. He is perceived by the line and other staff managers as possessing *high relative influence* in the decision-making process, or alternatively, as enjoying the support and confidence of top management.
3. His position and influence are perceived by the line and other staff

managers as resting upon his *professional expertise*, as opposed to his location in the organizational hierarchy.

4. He views the *organization as a totality* and perceives himself as being rewarded for the performance of the organization as a whole, as opposed to the output of his staff alone.
5. He encourages the resolution of conflicts arising in the course of the planning process among the departments, by bringing the conflicts out into the open and *confronting* them.

The study was conducted in four divisions, two each from two large corporations. These divisions will be referred to here as divisions A, B, C, and D. These divisions were chosen according to (1) the nature of the environment, and (2) the effectiveness of the planning process. Prior researches had shown that the nature of the environment affected the degree of structure of an organization, and might influence the task of integration; therefore, two divisions (A and B) were chosen from more certain environments, and two (C and D) from less certain environments.[3] The second criterion, effectiveness of the planning process, was assessed on the basis of data on the following aspects: commitment to and participation of division personnel in planning, resolution of conflict in preparing the plan, and use made of the plan documents. According to these qualifications, divisions B and D seemed to have relatively more effective planning processes, and divisions A and C less effective ones.

The Planner's Integrative Role

The findings which follow are necessarily limited by the small size of the sample, and therefore are more in the nature of strong tendency than of finality. However, the study provided substantial support for our first hypothesis that emergent planning departments had a key integrative role to play. The corporate planner of one of the two companies explained the integration problem as follows:

Since 1958 this company has gone through a phase of extreme decentralization from one of extreme centralization. During this period, also, its product lines have expanded vastly beyond the traditional items. Till recently it had a very thin corporate staff to deal with the massive geographic and product line diversity. In 1959 a Corporate Controller came in, and in 1963 were appointed chiefs of Marketing Services, R & D, and Personnel.

---

[3] The significance of this term and a way of assessing it, due to Lawrence and Lorsch, are discussed later in this chapter.

This helped, but was not enough. . . . From a seemingly high liquidity in 1968, the company has also been running into a resource constraint; the vise is tightening. Meantime, the opportunities in the market place have increased tremendously. Each division would like to reach the moon. The company is like a kid in the candy shop. You have to have a corporate-wide picture and coordinated decision-making to make the right trade-offs. This picture has to have a long term perspective. It is here, I think, that I can make the most significant contribution by making it easier for the top operating officers of this company to think in these terms.

One of the divisional managers commented as follows:

In the last few years this division has been the fastest growing one in this company. As part of this growth, you also get into programs with newer and more different technological bases. It is then very easy for people to live in their little worlds and know nothing about what is going on outside each little world. But if you sit in the driver's seat and want the division to head some place, you want to make sure these guys pull together. By hindsight, I can see that is why we needed a Division Planning Committee. We've since come a long way. Much depends on the planner. To me, he should be a "disinterested" professional, and a fellow who can talk to all the other fellows. It he is, he can play a unique role in coordination. He supplements the efforts of this management, and should have our full support.

Managers in all the divisions believed that the control system based on decentralized profit centers generated certain centrifugal forces, and they hoped that planning could overcome some of these forces, or at least neutralize their dysfunctional effects. The budget, as a "commitment in blood," encouraged a narrow as well as a short-run point of view, at the expense of overall divisional and long-term interests. By facilitating thinking over a wider horizon and a longer time span, the planner was in a position to help improve organizational effectiveness.

The data also provided some clues on certain special features of the planner's integrative responsibilities. This can perhaps be seen in a sharper light by contrasting the planner's integrative role with the, by now, more traditional integrative roles of the new product coordinator or the programme managers. In terms of the differentiation-integration model we have so far implicitly been speaking of "horizontal" integration, meaning lateral coordination of functional subsystems more or less on the same hierarchical level, such as the role played by the new product coordinator in bringing together the research, sales, and manufacturing departments in the development of new product ideas.

But in formulating long-term goals, strategies and action programmes based on internal and external environmental forecasts and analyses, different levels of the organizational hierarchy have to be involved. Information and communication in the form of comments, suggestions, questions, and instructions have to flow up and down. The planner's job is to facilitate such flow and interaction. This may be termed "vertical" integration. It means that the planner should be able to feel comfortable in different "worlds"—the world of top management, as well as the worlds below. A major component of his job is bringing together corporate management and the division general managers. Similarly, the division planner has to interact with, and bring about interaction between, the division top management and the "field" management, in order to facilitate a parallel divisional-departmental exchange. Thus, in addition to the horizontal integrative role, the planner's job includes an element of vertical integration.

Another unique feature seems to be that the planner's integrative role has both a longer formation and a longer gestation period. The product coordinator enters a somewhat better defined problem situation in dealing with Research, Sales and Manufacturing, and his efforts are generally related to a relatively shorter span of time. But the introduction of long-range planning itself generally poses a change problem, the solution of which takes some time. It is probably only after the successful completion of the change process that the planner can begin to be effective in his integrative role. During the change process he would, hopefully, have established the viable change relationships, which would give him the basis on which to assume more and more integrative responsibility. Also, the planner's integration of lateral subsystems and vertical hierarchical levels is done in a long-term perspective, so that his contribution in this role would also have a longer time span.

Determinants of Effectiveness

Given the significance of the integrative aspect of the planner's job, we were interested in the factors which would further the effectiveness of the planner's integrative contribution. Our first hypothesis concerning attributes and skills of the planner was that an orientation towards time and task intermediate to those of other organization members would make the planner a more effective integrator. We felt that such intermediacy would enable the planner to find more meeting ground with people on either side and thus facilitate collaboration between them.

Each respondent was asked to indicate the percentage of his time spent on matters that would show up in the income statement during

FIGURE 10.1
Time Orientations

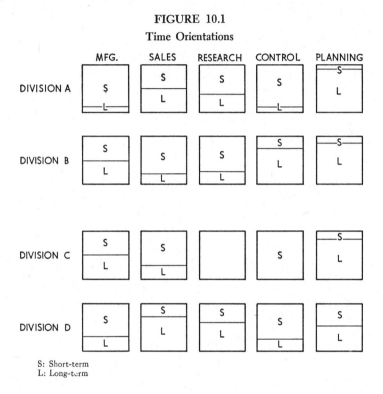

S: Short-term
L: Long-term

four different time periods, ranging from "one quarter or less" to beyond five years.

Except in Division D, planners showed a markedly greater long-term orientation than their counterparts in the other subsystems (Figure 10.1.) Also, the averages of the scores on long-term orientation for the other departments were computed and the deviation of planning scores from the average were as follows: Division A—69%; Division B—40%; Division C—56%; and Division D—4%. Since the smallest deviations are found in the two divisions with the more effective planning departments, this suggests that an intermediate time orientation is in fact desirable if the planner is to be effective.

Concerning task orientation, respondents were asked to rank ten considerations that might arise in the course of preparing the plan. The ten considerations were divided between production, marketing, and research concerns. The actual scores for each concern for each of the five subsystems by division were computed. (Figures 10.2A and 10.2B).

The scores of planners in the divisions with the more effective

FIGURE 10.2A

Task Orientations

DIVISIONS A & B

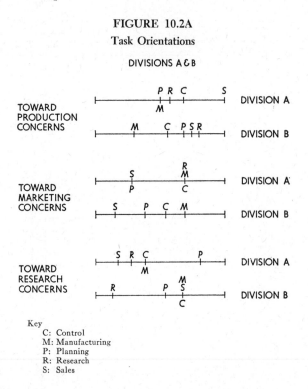

Key
    C: Control
    M: Manufacturing
    P: Planning
    R: Research
    S: Sales

planning departments, B and D, fall notably closer to an intermediate point between the other subsystems than scores for divisions A and C, which consistently fall on either extreme point. The data therefore indicate that the planner's intermediate task orientation also contributes to his effectiveness.

Relative Influence and Basis of Position

Our second hypothesis was that the planner who was seen as having high relative influence in the decision-making process was

FIGURE 10.2B

Task Orientations

DIVISIONS C & D

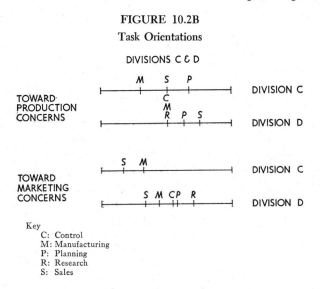

Key
  C: Control
  M: Manufacturing
  P: Planning
  R: Research
  S: Sales

likely to be more effective. Consequently, the respondents were asked to indicate, using a five-point scale, how much say or influence they thought each department had on the following six aspects:

Setting divisional goals;
Formulating divisional strategy;
Acquisitions;
Reconciliation of possible conflicts in projections made by Sales, Research, and Production;
The final draft of the plan;
Major capital projects.

The "relative influence" indices computed from these responses were not in support of our hypothesis. The indices were higher for planners in divisions A and C, while the planning processes in these divisions were thought to be less effective.

Looking back, however, it appears that perhaps the phrasing of this section might have led the respondents to interpret the word "influence" to mean something like "authority." What we really tried to get at might be termed "stature," in the sense of being a recognized and respected voice on the aspects of planning under consideration. Also, the six aspects listed are items which are not always dealt with explicitly or through an observable mechanism in the organization. Respondents might have felt distant from these aspects, and because of their unfamiliarity with such activities, they might have thought that the planner was "wired in" to the top. Besides, the "influence" attributed to the planners of Divisions A and C did not seem to correspond to the actual situation. Division A planner described his position partly as follows:

I find it very difficult to get his (the divisional general manager's) time for planning. In the first few months he did not even seem to take notice of my being here. I was not invited to his meetings. Things have improved since then, but not greatly. He still gives ten times as much attention to the budget: the others here naturally get the message and follow his lead.

The situation in Division C was very similar.

These contradictory pieces of evidence suggest that perhaps the planner's being perceived as occupying a position of "power" may detract from his effectiveness.

We next hypothesized that the planning process would be more effective if the planner's position and influence were based on his professional expertise, rather than on his hierarchical position. (At this point in our discussion, however, "stature" seems to be a more relevant term than "influence".) By the term "professional expertise" we mean the planner's familiarity with the body of knowledge relevant to his job of planning. This expertise includes the types, frameworks, and methodologies of planning, familiarity with the growing literature on planning, as well as a certain intimate knowledge of the division's business, in order to be able to choose and apply appropriate concepts in different circumstances. We do not mean that the planner should know the line manager's job better than the manager does, or that he should second-guess him. Still, the planner must not only possess this expertise, but show that he knows how to use it.

Comments of division executives in Divisions B and D, the divisions with the more effective planning processes, implied that the positions of planners probably rested substantially on their professional expertise. For example, the managers of Manufacturing Services in Division B said:

The Division General Manager occasionally refers to the planning people as "procedural professionals." I think this is a very descriptive phrase. Without the planner, I doubt that the concept and discipline of planning would have sunk in in this division as well as they have. It is not a matter of issuing edicts.

According to the vice president for advanced technology in Division D:

The engineer's tendency here is to view each defense program from which we expect to receive some business as a separate piece. But you can't do much by way of planning for unspecified future programs; you have a better handle if you think in terms of the areas in which this division has competence. Bob (the planner) has been patiently trying to get across just this concept of "business areas." It's tough. But, besides his knowledge of "planning theories," Bob has a few other things going for him. With his exposure to both Engineering and Marketing, he has a pretty good grasp of our business.

In the two divisions with the less effective planning processes, the planners contributions were not seen as valuable by managers from other departments, regardless of their actual expertise. For instance, the Division A sales managers observed:

Last year we were told that the economy would keep on expanding. Even a few months ago the people here were still singing its praise. Then auto sales dropped and the stock market started to skid. I am going to wait and see how good these crystal gazers are. . . .

We make these five year sales projections. They are made by product line and model. The figures beyond the second year don't mean much, and I don't care for them. But because the planner is on our trail, we have to dream them up. They may be useful to someone else downstairs, perhaps in the treasurer's office. . . .

In Division C the planner himself was aggressive and hard-working. But the enormously detailed approach, using a computer program and leading to a "credibility gap" in the plan, appeared to have shaken the division executives' confidence in the planning methodology. He also tended to project a rather strong line image and point of view during the field work for the plans.

Perceived Bases for Reward

Our fourth hypothesis was that the planning process is likely to be more effective if the planner views the organization as a totality and believes that he is being rewarded for the performance of the organization as a whole. With this idea in mind we asked the division managers to choose from among six possible bases for performance evaluation, the three that they considered *most desirable* and rank them in order of their desirability. Next they were asked to choose the three bases that seemed *actually* most important and rank them in order of importance. The following six bases were listed:

My own individual accomplishment
The output of the Planning Department
How well I get along with members of the other departments
The improvements effected in the sophistication and refinement of the planning techniques
The extent to which the plan helps the division achieve management's objectives
How well I get along with my superiors

TABLE 10.1

Perceived Bases of Reward

Basis \ Division	A	B	C	D
OVERALL desirability score	11	6	8	7
OVERALL importance score	9	6	9	7
AVERAGE of the two overall scores	10.0	6.0	8.5	7.0

In order for the managers to support our hypothesis, the managers would have to choose the following three bases out of the six, in the given order:

1. The extent to which the plan helps the division achieve management's objectives
2. The improvements effected in the sophistication and refinement of the planning techniques
3. How well I get along with the members of the other departments

Our idea was that the planner should have a global point of view, and that he should perceive his rewards as being given for working with others for the achievement of superordinate goals. In the bases listed above (1) refers to such superordinate goals, (2) refers to means of contributing to the goals, and (3) refers to an "other-directed" divisional orientation. The other three bases related to a more circumscribed point of view; in effect, the six items were divided between "division-centered" and "department-centered" orientations.

The overall desirability and actual scores, as well as the average of these two scores, as estimates of the "perceived" bases of reward, are shown in Table 10.1. With our scoring method, a small score would indicate a relatively greater division-centered orientation on the part of the planner. The minimum possible score is 6 and the maximum possible score is 12.

The above data are shown in diagramatic form in Figure 10.3.

These results show that the planners of Divisions B and D are much more division-centered than the planners in the other two divisions. Division A planners appear to be particularly department-centered in their orientation; Division B, on the other hand, is as

FIGURE 10.3

Perceived Bases of Reward

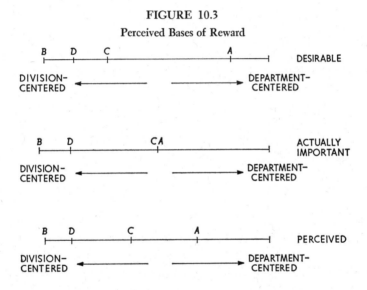

close to the division-centered orientation as is possible with our instrument. Since Divisions B and D have the most effective planning processes, these results provide substantial support for our hypothesis that the effective planner's view must include the entire organization.

Conflict Resolution in Planning

Our final hypothesis was that the planning process is likely to be more effective if the planner encourages conflict resolution by facilitating open confrontation. The data we gathered pertaining to this hypothesis showed that Divisions B and D made relatively greater use of confrontation in the resolution of conflicts in the course of planning, but the differences were not found to be statistically significant. Our data did indicate, however, that perhaps the actual method of confronting issues is different among the two pairs. For example, in Divisions A and C, the conflict resolution system tended to oscillate, somewhat sharply, between confrontation and forcing, or between confrontation and smoothing. In other words, if confrontation didn't work, the planners resorted to forcing or smoothing. In the other two divisions, B and D, a moderate positive correlation between confrontation and smoothing implied to us a more positive, problem-solving type of confrontation. We concluded that in Divisions B and D, the parties confronting one another did not see the situation so much as a win-lose situation as did Divisions A and C managers.

In summary, although the sample is very small and our limited data did not always show up statistically significant differences between the divisions, we are able to sum up certain factors which contribute to the greater effectiveness of the B and D divisional planning processes. These factors can be listed as planner characteristics: intermediate task orientations; perceived high position based on professional expertise (which has been demonstrated as operationally useful); and a global, divisional point of view.

ENVIRONMENT AND THE PLANNER'S
INTEGRATIVE ROLE

We observed earlier that planning departments seem to be a response to the integrative needs arising from environmental complexity. So the nature of the environment has a significant influence on the magnitude of the integration task in an organization.

This influence is felt through the impact of the environment on organizational structure. Structure is predicted to be inversely related to the degree of "certainty" of the environment. Three indices of "certainty" suggested by Lawrence and Lorsch are management's perceptions of:

1. The rate of change of environmental conditions
2. The certainty of information at any point in time about environmental conditions
3. The time span of definitive feedback from the environment.

In general, the higher the rate of change, the more uncertain the information, and the longer the time span of feedback, the greater the uncertainty.

Now, in a firm with a relatively more certain environment, its organization tends to be more structured. Integration in this sort of firm would be relatively easy. Conversely, for a firm with a less certain environment, the consequent low structure would imply difficulty in integration. Therefore, as we stated earlier, we believe that the integrative role of the firm would be relatively more important if the firm's environment was relatively *less* certain. Our Divisions A and B were chosen from relatively more certain environments and Divisions C and D from relatively less certain environments.

Our data supported the relationship between environmental characteristics and organizational structure predicted in the literature.[4] They also suggested that the integrative role was of relatively greater importance in an organization facing a relatively less certain environment. This seems to happen for two reasons. First, the degree of subsystem differentiation in such an organization is higher, and hence the need for "lateral" (or horizontal) integration is greater. Second, the greater need to facilitate intercourse between top management, on the one hand, and operating management, closer to the environmental boundary on the other, increases the importance of the "vertical" integrative component of the planner's job.

Guidelines for Planners

The things we have been talking about—the division of labor and the structuring of organizations on the basis of such division—are not new developments. But viewing organizations explicitly as total systems, made up of differentiated subsystems that need to be integrated for effective organizational performance, is extremely helpful in the study of organizational design and control. Top managements by themselves cannot adequately cope with the integration needs of increasingly complex organizations. New organizational subsystems emerge to share the integrative tasks, and among these are the planning departments.

In drawing implications for the planner's integrative role, it seems

---

[4] See, for example, James S. Garrison, "Organizational Patterns and Industrial Environments," (unpublished doctoral dissertation, Harvard University Graduate School of Business Administration, 1966).

inevitable that the planner have a longer term orientation, simply by the nature of his job. The difficulty, however, is that people in the functional departments are likely to be concerned more with day-to-day operations. The usefulness of a long-term plan may not be obvious to these people. It would therefore behoove the planner to get involved in their short-term concerns at first, and then gradually begin to point out the advantages of a longer term perspective in certain matters.

We found that the planner's intermediate task orientation did enhance his effectiveness, but we are also aware that such an orientation calls for a certain detachment and objectivity on the planner's part, as well as an impartial attitude toward the various functional concerns. An intermediate task orientation does not, of course, mean that the planner should spend "equal" time on the various functions, especially since certain functions may be more critical at certain times than others. But he should try to promote an image of the impartial helper, willing to devote extra attention to an individual function when necessary.

In order to prevent himself from over-identifying with certain concerns, the planner might try to constantly keep top management's point of view before him. He should do this, however, in a way which does not smack of power to operating personnel. A divisional orientation would also lead the planner to perceive the value of his work as it contributes to total organizational performance.

Hopefully, the planner will possess not only professional expertise, but an intimate knowledge of the division's business. We found that he is likely to be more effective if this is true. Operating merely from a position of formal authority is likely to impair the planner's effectiveness, and we, therefore, advise the planner to avoid being identified with the top power structure, and instead to earn his position and leverage through the demonstrated usefulness to the division and subsystems of the points of view and methodologies he has to offer.

Such a knowledge-based position will also help him articulate and re-interpret the potential and overt conflicts which are inevitable in the course of planning. He is in a position to encourage a problem-solving type of confrontation of such differences. One way to do this is through a division Planning Committee, but in the absence of such a formally named device, the planner can simply try to bring about as many interactions between the concerned subsystems as is necessary and feasible. Success, however, depends upon the planner's being able to demonstrate the value of these interactions. He can serve this end during discussions by clarifying and re-stating the issues involved from the various functional points of view, and by feeding in the needed information.

Our recognition of the relation of the environment to the planning job goes counter to a frequently unstated assumption in current literature and practice that there is "one best way" to approach the planning function. Planners perhaps tend to see themselves as occupying an "organizational box," where their job is to see that as much of the "theory of planning" as possible is applied in the organization. The above recognition would call for a move away from such a "box" and a new awareness of the organization's particular environment by the planner.

Guidelines for Management

We have talked about the increasing need for integration in large organizations, and also about the fact that top managements are finding their own time and resources more and more inadequate to meet this need. Our research indicates that planning could prove invaluable in taking some of the integrative load off top management's shoulders. Since we have found that an intermediate task orientation is advantageous for the planner, and since it is reasonable to assume that, in general, persons belonging to one of the existing functional subsystems may not possess such intermediacy, we conclude that it is desirable to appoint some one as a full-time planner.

Having appointed a planner, management must realize that the planner will be more successful in his integrative role if he enjoys their confidence and support, without seeming to be "powerful." The planner should be in a position to facilitate interaction between the top and lower levels of management—not to substitute for top management.

Management can further ensure the realization of the integrative potential of planning by making it clear, by its words and deeds, that it evaluates and rewards the planner for the extent to which planning helps goal-oriented action in the organization. The planner will thus be motivated to be less concerned with his own specialty and more with organizational results.

In tapping the potential of planning, management can also help by providing leadership in the resolution of conflicts. This does not mean that they should force issues to the breaking point, but that they should encourage a patient and solution-oriented exploration of the issues. With an overview of the division, and a certain intellectual independence, the planner is in a good position to be catalyst in the above process. But his may well be a cry in the wilderness without management's support, based on the faith that positive confrontation can be functional. One way to demonstrate this support is to set up a procedural mechanism which will provide opportunities for the meeting of minds between the organizational subsystems, with the planner as a full and valued participant in the working of the mechanism.

We mentioned earlier that a good planner must keep out of an organizational "box," and explicitly take cognizance of the environment as a variable affecting his job. If he is to be successful, management must share this view.

It behooves a planner to draw attention to possible discrepancies in the emergent structure and the structure that would seem appropriate on the basis of environmental demands. Management, in its turn, may do worse than authorizing a fuller investigation of such a discrepancy. The planner himself is not an expert designer of organizations. But he is probably in a good position to state some of the demands that deliberately planned changes will make on structure. It is for management to assume the responsibility for making strategic decisions to effect structural changes, should they be needed. For, if one does not change in a changing environment, one is liable to be left behind.

11 | Synergy as the Optimization of Differentiation and Integration by the Human Personality

Charles Hampden-Turner

This chapter is an essay, not a research report. It is included in this volume of research studies to provide perspective of a particular kind. It addresses the idea behind the D & I model of organization from a psychological and even a philosophical standpoint. It provides help in understanding how the logical opposites of differentiation and integration can be creatively combined to produce a whole that is greater than the sum of the parts. Charles Hampden-Turner, its author, is a man who is difficult to place in any convenient professional category. This article suggests to the reader not only why this is true but also that he is a gifted writer with a passion for ideas. He has a book in process that further develops these ideas, *Radical Man: The Process of Psycho-social Development*. He is currently a Research Fellow with the Cambridge Institute.

S YNERGY is a word deriving from the Greek "syn" meaning "with," "ergo" meaning "work." It literally means "to work with." The parts of an organization are said to be *synergistic* when the departments or various functions optimize one another, so that the whole becomes *more* than the parts.

Synergy may be physical as when all the components, plus labor, plus skillful assembly combine to produce a product which does *more* than the separate parts. An example would be a television set. Synergy can be economic as when the cost of the components, labor, etc., combine to form a product of greater economic value, than the mere addition of the parts. All living things are examples of biological synergy. No list of ingredients, no analysis of chemical make up can tell us why an organism grows, and why it defies, at least temporarily, the laws of entropy. Life is a very peculiar *state of organization* and death is precipitated, first and foremost, by a breakdown of this organization.

What will concern us in this essay is psychological synergy, or more broadly, psycho-social synergy. There is a psychological basis to all synergies related to animal life. Hence unless our television set had been well designed by a creative human mind, neither the physical nor the economic synergies could have come to pass.

Suppose for instance that I was a physicist from another planet without the benefits of television and upon visiting earth I was confronted by a television set. Now all knowledge of all physics on this earth and the other could not avail me in comprehending what manner of thing this was, *unless I knew the purpose of its creator,* or the values sought and consummated by the operation of the mechanism.

This illustration goes to show that psychological synergy is ultimately normative. How a television set *ought* to work, the conception of "good television" and the mutual understanding of these terms by human beings is essential to the physical, economic and corporate synergies which can only be built on an ideal or moral conception.

The concept of synergy is not too popular with many hard scientists, statisticians or computor experts. Why? Partly because it is "value full" rather than value free and partly because it has a tricky way of eluding mathematical computation. You cannot add together the parts because the whole point of synergy is that the whole is *more* than the parts. You cannot even multiply the parts with each other because synergy produces qualitative changes not present in the separate ingredients. The whole basis of mathematics is that numbers must be commutative and associative. That is, 1 and 2 and 3 are the same as 3 and 2 and 1, or 2 and 1 and 3, etc. But in creative, living and synergistic processes the way you associate the parts makes *all* the difference. 1, 2, 3 may be a living combination producing 10, which is more than its additives, while 3, 2, 1 may be a diseased and disintegrating combination.

While no one as ignorant of mathematics as I would dare to predict that it will never embrace synergistic transferences, it certainly cannot do so at the moment and so we are faced with the problem of thinking about synergy in largely qualitative terms. Psychological synergy may be either conceptual or emotional, but is usually both.

Let us take first a conceptual example. Consider Gutenberg's invention of the printing press. He had seen molten coins poured into a mold. He had watched a die stamp make the impression on the face of the coin. He had seen carved wooden blocks used to stamp playing cards. Yet none of these solved his problem of how to produce hundreds of bibles for a pilgrimage—until he saw a wine press operating. Then, by a creative recombination of old images, he selected the molten metal and the die from the coin stamp, the flat beds from the wine-press, and the ink stamping mechanism from the manufacture of playing cards. "A simple substitution . . . God hath revealed to me the miracle." Now a printing press may be "nothing more" than the recombination of old images but in this case the "more" revolutionized the medieval world and precipitated both the Renaissance and the Protestant Reformation.

But synergy can also be emotional. How competent we feel at work, or how loved at home, depends largely upon the response we evoke in others and the response others invoke in us. When Romeo says to Juliet, "the more I give you the more I have," he is testifying to the synergistic and accumulative nature of emotional strength and energy in human relationships. In practice emotional and conceptual synergy are usually combined. A communicates a meaningful idea to B, who responds enthusiastically with an elaboration and qualification of the idea, which in turn enthuses A. When the two men part company subsequently both take away with them more emotional energy, feelings of well-being, and more complex thought-matrices than either possessed prior to the interaction.

Synergy can endlessly multiply itself, increasing its strength and elaborating its quality. Hence if A and B have formed a synergistic relationship, each can return to their own families and communicate what they have learnt to A1, A2, A3, B1, B2, and B3. Then these persons will find their personal resources enhanced and in turn will be better enabled to form synergistic relationships with others.

Of course the continuation of synergy will depend on the communicative skill of the persons involved as well as the content of what is communicated. Once during a demonstration against the Anglo-French invasion of Suez I was struck hard upon the head by a banner labeled "Don't Use Force." Ever since it has concerned me that the synergistic content of a communication may be contradicted by its manner of delivery. And of course the person who receives a message labeled "love" which none the less reduces and cripples his sense of competence is likely to become schizophrenic, authoritarian or worse, since he loses his capacity to associate correctly symbols with experience.

But what has synergy to do with differentiation and integration? Quite simply, synergy *is the optimal integration of that which was formerly differentiated.* Now the previous state of differentiation is extremely important. If Gutenberg wanted to print Bibles for a pilgrimage, what the hell was he doing playing with cards, coins, and wine-presses? A strict moralist would almost certainly have berated him for letting his mind wander to such drunken, mercenary, and frivolous topics (almost as bad as Pascal shooting dice, and Ben Franklin flying a kite—at his age!). But what made these synergies so climactic and significant, was the very *remoteness* of the original thought-matrices. Indeed we call a person "creative" precisely because he has combined things we never thought of combining. Had Gutenberg made it a habit never to associate with such unholy persons as wine merchants or the manufacturers of playing cards, he would not have created a synergy that transformed civilization. Only if persons of sufficiently differentiated viewpoints come together can their integration reach high levels of synergy. Where I get together with persons very similar to myself, the same company, the same department, the same town, the same school, the same age, etc., then the likelihood of adding significant dimensions to my mind, through ingesting thoughts novel to my experience, is very small.

Emotional synergy follows the same rule. An important part of being a male animal is the capacity to attract and please a female. The differentiation between male and female is quite crucial to their successful integration. Consider the effect of overpowering and dominating one's female partner until she becomes the mere echo of one's own thoughts and sentiments. In thus destroying her individuality and differentiation from oneself one also destroys the significance of her approval or love. Who is comforted or inspired by a mere echo? If *her separate* life is not enhanced by *your separate* life, no genuine synergy has been achieved.

Or take another example of two men in professional roles who are not sufficiently differentiated. A is a purchasing officer who actually hates his job but values the prestige of his high income. B is a professional footballer who regards the sport as a racket, but feels he can really make money for a few years. When A and B meet they are not likely to widen each other's perspectives, since they are both narrowly concerned with money, but they are also unlikely to find emotional rapport, because if B earns more than A, the latter will feel *inferior* to him. As Gilbert and Sullivan put it, "When everybody's somebody, then no one's anybody."

This is *only* true when A and B value exactly the same thing and one has more of this same thing than the other. In this event *the success of one will always entail the relative failure of the other*. But if A and B value *different* qualities so that A really enjoys and excels at purchasing and B feels exhilarated every time his hands or feet touch leather, then there is every chance that their relationship could be synergistic. Each could learn from the other about business or football, and neither need feel subordinate to the other since their skills are not really comparable. The fact that B is the world's greatest footballer in no way eclipses or reduces the need for or the value of A's purchasing activities.

The examples given here may sound very simple and obvious but the theme of differentiation and synergistic integration which underlies them is of considerable importance and is very widely ignored in the discourse of experts. The most immediate reaction to differentiation and integration by those schooled in formal logic is that they are opposites. The more differentiated you are the less integrated you will be. The scores on one dimension should be substracted from scores on the other. In research we should therefore devise a differentiation-integration continuum and locate various persons somewhere between the two polarities. In programming a computer, $D = 0$ and $I = 1$ and ne'er the twain shall meet.

Now this view is not entirely wrong. If we took all the children who had rebelled against their parents, we might well find that the integration of their families was poorer, than those of nonrebels. But the view is very wrong in one respect, for it overlooks the fact that D and I *in the right proportions* are synergistic. Hence Paul Lawrence and Jay Lorsch found in their research that *on the whole*, the more widely differentiated subsystems in a company were less well integrated, and *on the whole* the less widely differentiated systems were better integrated, but that the most successful companies of all were widely differentiated *and* well integrated.

The oppositional tendency of D and I and the synergistic tendency of D and I would seem to depend upon their relative proportions in any relationship. A similar principle is at work in the Managerial Grid Seminars designed and organized by Blake and Mouton (1964). They contend that concern with people (an integrative orientation) and concern with the several functions of productivity (a differentiating orientation) can be optimized. A poor manager is essentially an "unbalanced" one or a "compromised" one. Unbalanced managers score disproportionately high on their concern with production *at the expense* of a concern with employees, or vice versa. Compromised managers find that every concession made to people subtracts from productivity and vice versa, so that they must "split the difference." But the good manager creates synergistic relationships not only between himself and others, but between the norms of high productivity and humanism *within his own mind*. Hence research which evaluated the results of "managerial grid" training in a Texas plant, found that *between* people the degree of individual and deviant expressions had increased (differentiation), yet relationships had also improved (integration). *Within* people the number of "soft" and hazy norms had given way to clearer, tougher and more *differentiated* views while at the same time an increased number of *integrated* norms were apparent.

This pattern closely resembles the research on *The Open and Closed Mind* by Milton Rokeach. Here it was found that the "open mind" consisted of a larger number of different ideas between which there was communication and mutual interdependence. The closed mind had relatively few ideas (low differentiation) and these were isolated, contradictory and compartmentalized (poor integration).

The question now arises, how can this optimum balance between D and I be created and maintained? One answer, suggested by the research studies, is that synergistic balance is best achieved by an egalitarian dialogue between the persons involved in the relationship. Only if all feel that their individuality is respected, as is their need to communicate and win approval, can the highest attainable degree of individuality (or differentiation) be combined with highest attainable degree of communication (or integration). No wonder then, that Lawrence and Lorsch found that "forcing" a decision unilaterally upon subordinates accompanied an imbalance between D and I.

One of the most common experiences of social life is that the most creative, individual, and complex people have the best chance of making a resounding impact on other people *and* the best chance of making a "dull thud." In other words, every man who dares to be different stands to excel by the same proportion as he stands to fail. The existential writer, Camus, stated, "I rebel, therefore we exist." It is equally true that the rebellious can become alienated and lost. For this reason every man suffers "basic uncertainty" or "existential anxiety" which *cannot be reduced,* without also reducing the chances of a higher synergy.

It follows that the balance between differentiation and synergistic integration is not a stable balance. Each thought, each man, each group, each corporation, can only *dare* to differentiate itself, that is to *un*balance itself, and then strive to *re*balance or reintegrate itself across the wider divide between it and others. The twinge of anxiety accompanies the inevitable fear of unbalance, of failing to reach the other because of an overly wide differentiation. With failure to reintegrate, *D and I immediately become oppositional instead of optimal.*

I believe we have a clue to the desperate need for synergy in society, when we encounter the highly emotional needs for "justice" which literally means "balance" and is symbolized by scales. Of course few agree about what is just and what is not. Since nearly all of us see our own concerns clearly and those of others dimly, the "judge in his own cause" who forces his self-serving decision on others is likely to be unjust. However people have risked all for their concept of justice and people can be outraged by an obvious injustice in their midst which does not directly concern them. The reason, I suggest, is that every synergy is, however remotely, connected to every other synergy. A society in which one man's perspective is stamped upon, can become rapidly unbalanced and tyrannical for all.

What is most new and unusual about the synergistic relationship between *D* and *I* is its total departure from Aristotelian logic, which divides the world into A and not-A and has been the basis of formal logic ever since. What Lawrence and Lorsch have shown us is the relevance of *dialectical logic* in which apparent opposites may suddenly become reconciled but only in "just" proportions.

We live in what is popularly referred to as an age of anxiety. We are suddenly all aware of fragmentation and alientation. The world seems endlessly divided and subdivided and in a permanent state of inadequate coordination. We spend billions on defending ourselves against other people and seem to exist on two planes, a technological maturity, and a psychological infancy.

The reason, I suggest, is that formal logic is differentiating in its assumptions and ramifications. It subordinates us to the laws of those instruments we ourselves created and the instruments branch out in ever accelerating patterns of technological innovation. The integrative task can only be achieved by dialectical logic which reconciles apparent contradictions. (In formal logic the presence of a contradiction signals a mistake! There is usually *one best way* given a consistent set of premises.)

In dialectical logic literally thousands of seeming contradictions and different needs are seen as potentially synergistic. Consider, for example, the many dichotomous structures and characteristics of the human personality. There is . . .

Dependency v. Autonomy	Conservative v. Radical
Extraversion v. Introversion	Intimacy v. Reflection
Tender minded v. Tough minded	Cooperation v. Individualism
Affiliation need v. Achievement need	Feminine v. Masculine
Flexibility v. Ego-Strength	Mutuality v. Rebellion
Open mindedness v. Conviction	Other-directed v. Inner-directed
Continuity v. Creativity	Involvement v. Detachment

These, of course, are only a very few of an almost endless list of dichotomies. By and large the left-hand column is usually associated with integrative functions, and the right-hand column is associated with differentiating functions. Now if D and I in just reconciliation are synergistic this should be true for our entire list of polarities with D and I themes.

The first thing to notice about this list is that nearly every polarity has a number of alternate words. Flexibility is generally regarded as good but "vacillation" and "wavering" sound bad. Similarly Ego-strength sounds desirable but "pride," "pig-headedness" are bad. Involvement is good, infatuation is bad. My conviction may be viewed by others as fanaticism or dogmatism.

All these gradations of good, bad, and neutral are used by us to signal to one another that the relationship has *too much* of one polarity as compared with the other, so that an imbalance is being presented.

If I think that in your behavior Involvement has overcome and overbalanced Detachment, I describe it as infatuation. If the situation, as I see it, calls for a definite stand and self-assertion (Ego-strength) but you continue to be so Flexible that no one knows what to expect, I accuse you of vacillation. In this way we constantly try and "nudge" each other's behavior into what is regarded as a synergistic balance, and in so doing we weigh the verdicts of several people against our own sense appropriateness.

Where synergy is achieved it involves not only the optimization of my needs with your needs, not only the optimization of D and I, but an Open Mindedness which increases and is increased by Conviction, a Creativity which maintains its essential Continuity, and Achievements which make my Affiliations stronger so that "men beat a path to my door."

In fact, synergistic vocabularies are gradually being invented. Persons who are tired of being "hung up" on the Dependency/ Autonomy polarity speak increasingly of autonomous interdependence. Norman Mailer tells us that he is a "conservative-radical," and existentialists say that we rebel in order to find a greater mutuality than we had before. Psychiatrists have started to say that a man should not be either introvert or extrovert but "alloplastic," i.e., in touch both with others *and* his own inner feelings. It is not difficult to see that if I know myself well this would help me comprehend all those who shared my human condition. In short there is not a single polarity in the list in which the two apparent opposites could not be optimally combined.

When we look at mental illness we see many varieties of over-differentiation or over-integration. Among neurotic symptoms are trembling, sweating, sexual impotence, excessive blushing, stammering, bed-wetting, facial tics and twitches, and all represent a kind of excessive autonomy by various parts of our body which cannot be brought under integrative and centralized control. But the neurotic can also suffer from overcontrol, lack of spontaneity, obsessive and retentative fixations, excessive tension, hyper-vigilance and self-conciousness. Frantic attempts at control seem to go hand in hand with loss of control. The victim typically "oversteers."

Among psychoses manic-depression is an obvious example of a shifting instability from a manic extroversion, an excessive attempt at integration, to a depressed introversion, and excessive attempt at differentiation.

Various groups and corporations will go through centralization and decentralization phases as the *D* and *I* pendulum swings back and forth. At one period everyone will be praising "individualism" and "creativity" and "tough decision-making," then the "good relations" school will get into the saddle for months or years until someone whispers "organization man," and the tender-minded are once more replaced by the tough-minded.

An entertaining satire on this process was contained in the musical "How to Succeed in Business without Really Trying." The hero engaged in skillful infighting and competitive differentiation, until the system was on the verge of disintegration and was full of desper-

196 Studies in Organization Design

ate anxieties. At precisely the right moment, the hero jumps on the table to sing "The Brotherhood of Man," and with tremendous relief and enthusiasm the whole social system swings over from its overly differentiated state to a highly integrated one.

It follows from these observations that the "Excellent Manager" would be a "synergist" who brought just the right proportions of his total personality resources to the situation. Faced with an unbalanced system and an unbalanced employee he would provide the missing emphasis which was sufficient to create synergy between them without "over-balancing" the situation.

What implications does this have for the development of personality? How could we recognize the manager who is most alive and developed? The answer must be that development consists of an interdependent growth in the saliency of all the polarities listed, and others. The developed manager is more autonomous *and* more interdependent, more extrovert when others are shy, but also more introverted and reflective about his extroversion. More open-minded, and because he has heard all sides before deciding, more convinced as a result. More creative and rebellious in his advocacy of new ideas, yet the ideas themselves and his skill can stabilize the boat which they initially rocked. His individualism would consist of better ways and ideas about cooperation.

While we generally expect the good manager to be self-stabilizing, the potential genius in a research laboratory may require the manager's help in becoming integrated. Because there is a division of labor within the company certain roles are inherently more differentiating and other roles are inherently more integrative. The genius is expected to go out on a limb and his deviance, and consequent anxiety and alienation, make strong demands for the "balancing" nature of the manager's support, nurturance and understanding.

In conclusion, I would only add that this power of synergistic reconciliation is the peculiar achievement of the human personality. Outside personality and living forms, all things are partial, dichotomized, separated and dead. Those who regard the world objectively and see it as apart from human needs and values, will seldom grasp the workings of synergy. Just as the genetic code passes instructions from cell to cell in our bodies and according to the quality of the instruction we grow, sicken, or die, so I believe moral codes, ideals, ideas, and concepts function similarly. They are coded instructions for growth or disaster. They can lead to progressively higher levels of D and I in all human systems, to slow atrophy, or to disaster.